Jack the Ripper

JACK THE RIPPER:
Newly Discovered Adventures of Sherlock Holmes

Holy Ghost Writer

Jack the Ripper

**Library of Congress Control Number:
2014918501 CreateSpace Independent
Publishing Platform, North Charleston, SC**
ISBN: 1502716984
ISBN-13: 978-1502716989

Jack the Ripper

Jack the Ripper

CONTENTS

Acknowledgment

Jack the Ripper

Jack the Ripper

ACKNOWLEDGMENTS

To Sir Arhur Conan Doyle, for the inspired creation of the greatest detective the world will ever know—Sherlock Holmes.

"When you have eliminated the impossible, whatever remains, no matter how improbable, must be the truth."

—Sherlock Holmes

Jack the Ripper

CHAPTER ONE
Fulfillment

"Polly! Polly, go upstairs like a good child. Mama's got company."

The little brown-haired girl picked up her doll and set of jacks and slowly climbed the weathered stairs leading up to her room. They creaked under her slight weight, and she took care to skip the board she knew was rotting. She glanced back and saw her mother pouring a glass of bourbon for a man who openly leered at her mother's slender figure, which was tightly corseted in her best silk dress. Polly was used to such scenes. Her mother had many male callers, but she never wanted Polly to meet any of them. For ten-year-old Polly, this was disturbing and confusing— though not as upsetting as the laughter and noises that would spill forth from her mother's bedroom in the middle of the night.

Polly's real name was Mary Ann Nichols, but her mother had called her Polly ever since Polly could remember; if someone had called her Mary Ann, it's unlikely she would have responded. Polly had never known her father; her mother said he had died when Polly was a baby. How she missed having a father, even if she was not sure quite what it felt like! She saw other young girls in public holding their fathers' hands, or swept up against a bearded cheek with affection, and it gave her a pain in her heart. If only father was alive, then her mother would act as a proper mother should, like other girls' mothers did—with civilized teas and household chores and directing the servants. But their household had no servants, and certainly no civilized teas.

In fact, Polly did not get to spend much time with her mother, who worked long hours at a factory. Instead, Polly spent most of her waking hours with Mrs. Johnson, the neighbor lady who kept her fed and clothed. Mrs. Johnson was a kind soul, but a little brusque, and she didn't fill the deep need Polly had for love.

On that afternoon, Polly sat down in front of her mirror, which was propped up on an old table in her bedroom. A roach crawled across the worn toe of her shoe, but Polly was used to the scuttling insects and did nothing more than twitch her foot. The roach flew into the wall and squeezed into a crack in the boards, moving on to safer territory.

Polly stared at herself and wondered what her life would be like in the future. She wanted a mother and a father who would love her. She wanted to be famous, like the beautiful woman she had seen on a poster outside of a theater. Then she would never feel like a burden—everyone would adore her and clamor for her company, and she would never be sent upstairs to spend hours alone. She was determined to make her life better as soon as she could, and after she was tired of being famous she would marry and have children of her own. Polly knew she would love her family, cook their meals, mend their clothes, and be respectable in a way her own mother would not. More importantly, having a family would mean she never had to be lonely—and it seemed she could not get any lonelier than she was now.

Suddenly, the image in the mirror shimmered and changed. Suddenly there sat Mary, as she preferred to be called now that she was past childhood, staring at the image of a mature woman. She had been lost in a reverie, looking back on her childhood dreams and memories. Polly had been sure her life would eventually be a charmed one—but Mary knew that adulthood was dreary and disappointing.

Her mother had died when Mary was only fifteen years old, and with no relations she was cast out onto the streets of Whitechapel. With no other way to survive, she was forced to follow in the footsteps of her mother and entertain gentlemen—she scoffed at that word now—for a living. She was forty-three with few possessions, fading beauty, and a lonely life in a second-rate boarding house. Occasionally a roach or a rat would pay her a visit, but no true friends ever darkened her doorstep. She laughed bitterly at this thought as she looked at the peeling paint on the walls and the water spots on the ceiling.

Her long dark hair was piled up on top of her head. The lines in her face showed what a hard life she had lived, but still she had hope that one day one of the many men in her life would fall in love with her and take her away from all of this. It had happened for other girls she knew—perhaps they had been younger than her, or more refined—but Mary refused to let go of the dream, however foolish it was. It was the only thing of value she had.

She poured herself a stiff drink of bourbon. Yes, she had inherited this habit from her mother as well. She often drank to excess, but the liquor dulled her pain and helped her get through the empty days and desperate nights.

This night, she would go to the local tavern and find a man—or perhaps more than one, if she was lucky—so that she could survive for a few more days. She had been ill and unable to work for nearly a week, and she hoped the shadows of the night would hide the bags under her eyes and how loosely her dress now fit.

She slipped into a low-cut black gown, which displayed her ample breasts and smooth shoulders. She then plastered on makeup to help cover up all of the lines and wrinkles and perhaps make herself appear a little younger. As the final touch, Mary put on a hat, wrapped a shawl around herself, and locked her door behind her.

A few hours later, she was still at the neighborhood pub, well on her way to being very drunk and smiling flirtatiously at any man who looked her way. She had already had three customers that night, all of whom she took to an alley outside, where they accomplished what they wanted and pressed a few greasy coins into her hand.

As a result, Mary finally had a little money in her purse, but she was spending it wildly on drinks. Perhaps it was the afternoon she had spent reflecting on her life, but Mary was desperate to dull the pain. She would certainly not come out ahead that night. When it appeared she could interest no one else, Mary sat with another woman at the bar; she was tired and almost too drunk to walk back to the boarding house. Realizing she needed to return home, she staggered out of the pub door.

Buck's Row in Whitechapel was a very seedy part of town—no one respectable dared step foot on that street. Drunks lined the sidewalks, and Mary was one of them that night. Several men propositioned her as she stumbled along, but she was too intoxicated and worn out to pay them any heed. She kept walking toward home, speaking briefly to friends or old clients she met on the way but determined to make it to her own bed. She did stop to share a smoke with a friend, Emily, who was none too sober herself.

"Mary, come back to my room," Emily slurred. "We'll have some coffee—you're in no condition to be on the streets."

Mary laughed at that. "Neither are you," she said. "Neither are any of us poor buggers who live this life. Another time, perhaps—another night."

Ten minutes later, on Friday, August 31,

1888, Mary would be dead.

She had turned away from the crowds, glad to finally have some peace, when a gentleman in a long trench coat, carrying a case, appeared in front of her. He was well-groomed, though his clothes were a little worn—at any rate, he had the confident look of a man with money. He was most decidedly out of place in a neighborhood frequented by unkempt sailors and blue-collar workers.

Mary decided she might have the energy for one more client when the man shoved her into an alley. She put out her hands to break her fall as she hit the pavement, and she dimly felt the sting of scraped palms. Some men liked their encounters with her rough— perhaps this fellow was the same, and she could charge him dearly for it. She clumsily started to pull up her skirts in preparation.

In her stupor, she was confused—that is, until she saw the glint of steel in the moonlight. Her confusion quickly turned to fear as she struggled with the man and tried to scream. He clamped his hand over her mouth to muffle her cries, although nobody would have noticed the noise or thought it unusual in that part of town.

Mary had finally made her mark in history,

destined to be remembered forever. She would become the first victim of Jack the Ripper, although she would not be around to enjoy that fame. The knife met its mark...twice in her throat, blood spurting all over her good black dress...and all of her thoughts disappeared. Her pitiful life was over.

CHAPTER TWO
Cased Curiosity

At 3:40 A.M., a delivery driver found Mary's mutilated body in the alley. Blood was everywhere, pooled thickly in the cobblestones—though in the darkness, it looked much like water. At first the driver thought the stiff figure on the ground was just a tarpaulin discarded by a tradesman or another worker. He edged closer and saw the mound of cloth was actually a woman, one whose skirt had been pulled over her head. He did not notice her throat had been cut, and he averted his eyes from her petticoats. He was certain the woman had been a common prostitute, but that was no reason to disrespect the dead.

Still, he thought to himself, *I don't know why it had to be me who found this body—I've got to finish my route. If I lose this job, I'll be the next one dead in the streets—at the hands of my own wife.* He jumped guiltily when another man entered the alleyway—suppose the newcomer thought he'd committed this vile deed?

"I turned the corner and came upon her like this," the delivery driver sputtered. "I haven't touched her—I haven't been here more than five minutes, I swear it."

The other man inched forward to examine the body, then raked his eyes over the delivery driver's lanky frame. "No need to worry," he said, waving his hand. "No call to think you did this—you'd be covered in blood."

"What should we do?"

"We?" asked the newcomer in surprise. "I'm going to work—what you do is no business of mine."

The delivery driver looked at his horse and buggy, and then back at the body. "I'll report it to the next police officer I see," he said. "I'm bound to run across one."

That being decided, both men left with clear consciences.

Police Constable Neil was walking his beat in the early hours of that morning—though the neighborhood was a rough one, he enjoyed the peace of it once all the drunks had fallen into their gutters and the whores had fluttered home. As he passed the alley where Mary's body was hidden, he perfunctorily shone his lantern down the passageway—and paused when he noticed the still form on the ground. Perhaps it was a drunk, passed out before she made it home;

regardless, it was his duty to investigate.

As he stepped slowly closer, his heavy boot slipped in a slick puddle of blood, and he almost fell against the woman. Recovering his balance, he leaned over and pushed aside the woman's heavy skirt from her face, recoiling at what he saw.

"My God," he gasped.

The woman's face was a death mask of horror and pain, and the bodice of her dress was soaked with blood. Neil immediately went for the local medic and coroner, Doctor Llewellyn, though he knew there was no hope for the poor creature before him.

When the other police arrived, the alley quickly became a scene of chaos and confusion. The coroner discovered that the two deep cuts on the sides of the woman's neck had lacerated all of the blood vessels. There was also a deep, jagged cut on her left side and seven smaller cuts on her right side. This woman hadn't felt these, for she had died almost instantly after her throat was slashed. She had bled out fairly quickly, thankfully.

The coroner also noticed that although the woman's legs were warm, her hands and feet were cold, telling him that she had been dead for only about thirty minutes. The police carried the body to the morgue for further examination, and the coroner went home to fortify himself with an earlier-than-usual shot of whiskey.

There had been an increased number of murders in the area lately, but most had been attributed to robberies and muggings gone awry. Now the authorities weren't so sure, but they did know this killer was a vicious one, based on the violence of the death and the disfigurement of the body afterward.

The strange murder was a source of interest for one man in particular: Sherlock Holmes. He had been keeping up with the news on a rash of killings in Whitechapel, but he had a particularly bad feeling about the most recent crime. News of the murder had reached the papers that morning and Holmes was sitting with his good friend, Dr. John Watson, discussing it.

"I believe this is a different murderer," he told Dr. Watson.

"How many murders have there been in the area so far?"

"Well, six I believe. But the others appear to be muggings—the bodies were found stripped of all valuables. The culprit did take something this time—but entrails are certainly not of monetary value," Holmes said. "And the killer also left a long cut across the victim's abdomen. There must have been a reason for it—especially if the poor girl was already dead. Why would a criminal suddenly go from mere robberies to mutilation?"

"Only a very sick and twisted individual would do such a thing," Dr. Watson replied. "But I would also surmise a person would have to know something about human anatomy to make such precise and purposeful cuts as this killer is reported to have made."

"Exactly my thoughts, as well. I'm most interested in this case—most interested."

"Is Scotland Yard going to consult with you? Solving difficult crimes is your forte, old friend," Dr. Watson said. "And we have not had a challenge in quite a while—this may be just the thing."

"I haven't heard from Scotland Yard yet, but that's not to say I won't. After all, this murder just happened. I would be more than happy to solve this puzzle, though, should they need help—and if they do not, I may even look into it on my own."

Mrs. Parker, Holmes' housekeeper, brought in two steaming cups of coffee. The men had settled into their respective chairs and both enjoyed puffs on their pipes, the sweet scent of tobacco filling the air. They were grateful for small pleasures after the disturbing news in the paper. This was the place where they always sat when Holmes relayed his stories to his friend and cohort—but this morning, there were no other stories than those of the dead woman.

Little did they know that Sherlock Holmes was being discussed at Scotland Yard's headquarters in Westminster at that very moment.

"Sherlock Holmes would be an asset to this investigation," Inspector Vincent Grant told his superiors firmly. "He often deals with the unusual, and he's one of the brightest minds in England. At the very least, he may have some opinion or see something we've missed in the evidence we've already collected."

It was agreed upon, and Inspector Grant left the office and headed for Holmes' residence. He had passed the neatly kept brick townhome many times, but had never had cause to call upon the famous detective at home until now. They had worked together before, however, and he was sure he would receive a cordial welcome.

Mrs. Parker answered the door, her apron crisp and her stature upright.

"Inspector Grant," he introduced himself. "I know I arrive unannounced and probably unexpected—I do hope it's convenient for Mr. Holmes to see me now. It's urgently important."

Mrs. Parker had overheard Holmes' and Dr. Watson's discussion that morning, and she knew Holmes would gladly welcome the inspector.

"This way to the study," she said as she led Grant through the house.

Holmes arose from his chair upon seeing the inspector and shook his hand. "Ah, my old friend! I'm glad you have come—I had hoped you would."

"How good to see you," Grant answered, "although you probably know why I am here. I wish it could be under better circumstances."

"Yes, I suspected you might need help on this new case of yours—I read all about it in the paper this morning. You remember my friend Dr. Watson, I am sure."

"Of course. How are you, Doctor?"

"Very well, thank you. Much better than you I must say, with your current case," Dr.

Watson answered. "It's a ghastly situation."

"Yes, it is," the inspector answered. "But we hope to catch the killer before he chooses another victim, if indeed he intends to."

Mrs. Parker brought in another cup of coffee as the inspector took a seat.

"Are you willing to come to the station with me and look over the evidence we've compiled so far?" Grant asked. "I would also like to take a trip to the morgue so you can view the body. I have never seen anything like this before—and Whitechapel is a rough place, where we have become accustomed to vile crimes."

"Of course, whatever you need me to do," Holmes answered. "I must say I am more than curious about this one."

The men discussed some of the particulars of the case, and Holmes told the inspector that he would meet him at the office after lunch.

"Thank you very much," Grant said as he finished his last sip of coffee and took his leave. "I will see you in a few hours. This may turn out to be your most challenging case yet."

Holy Ghost Writer

CHAPTER THREE
Devil's in the Details

Scotland Yard looked the same as it always had—an impressive brick façade looming over a busy road. Inside, dozens of people milled about, cigarettes hanging from their mouths as they busied themselves with some errand or another. Many of the faces seemed younger than Holmes remembered, but time marches on, he reminded himself. And it took a certain kind of man, one with a soul of steel, to survive long at Scotland Yard.

Holmes was led to Inspector Grant's office by a blonde secretary and told to wait there and to make himself comfortable.

"Would you like a cup of tea?" the woman asked.

"That would be very nice, thank you."

The young woman slipped through the door, leaving him alone for the moment. Holmes looked over the office. It had once been his, before he retired from the establishment and started taking on only the cases that most interested him. There had been many crimes solved within these walls…and still were, he was sure. There were certainly times he missed being swept up in the bustle of the agency, but all in all peace suited him better now.

He watched as Inspector Grant walked his way, stopping every now and then to sign a paper or answer a question. He was a busy man, and well-respected by his peers. He finally made it to the office and promptly shut the door. The men shook hands and they both took a seat; Grant behind the desk, Holmes in front of it.

"I want to thank you again for coming," Grant said to Holmes. "I am sure I interrupted you in something—I hope it was nothing too pressing."

"Oh, it is no bother at all. I am anxious to hear about the evidence that your men have gathered. Please tell me everything you know so far—I know we discussed the case at some length at my home, but I want to hear every detail. You never know what small clue can lead to a revelation!"

"I think we should walk over to the morgue first so you can see the victim. Then we can delve into the facts of the case as we know them. Let me send a messenger, so the coroner can arrange the body for viewing."

"Certainly."

When Grant had sent his messenger, the men got up and left for the morgue—it was only a short distance away, and the crisp fall air made for an invigorating walk. When they arrived, Donald Hamilton, the coroner's assistant, ushered them into the back room where the bodies were stored. The coroner met them there a few moments later.

"How do you do, Dr. Llewellyn?"

"Very well, thank you—and you, sir?"

"As well as can be expected, given the debauchery I see daily," answered Grant. "I would like you to tell Detective Holmes about Mary—he has a brilliant mind and is most eager to help solve this case."

"Of course," Dr. Llewellyn said as he moved to one of the tables and pulled back the sheet to reveal the victim.

Holmes, though he had seen many a body in his day, never got used to seeing those tale-tell autopsy stitches. He also never liked to see a body on a slab; perhaps it made him face his own mortality, but whatever the reason he knew he could never be an undertaker. The woman had been cleaned up and lay there as if she were asleep—that is, if you only looked upon her face.

"Her throat was cut twice; also her stomach

was cut open and she was disemboweled," the coroner said as he pulled the sheets further back and showed the detectives. "Part of her intestines were laid up on her shoulder. Why, I can only wonder. The murderer must have been in a hurry. This one took his souvenir with him, but not the type of souvenir that we have seen in these other murders—those were clearly robberies."

"Yes, body parts are usually not the normal thing to take," answered Holmes. "Did you find any other evidence around the scene—perhaps the murderer left something behind?"

"No, we did not. And the body was fairly clean except for the woman's own blood and a broken fingernail," the coroner said as he motioned to the woman's right index finger. The nail had been torn off down to the quick. She still had a hint of red lipstick on her lips, which made the scene all the more surreal and grotesque.

"I assume, given her dress and grooming, that she was—ahem—a lady of the night?" Holmes asked. "I apologize if the question is indelicate."

"We are all adults here," answered the coroner. "And we know many such women in the city survive on the streets—the question is not an indelicate one. Yes, she made her living in the way you suggest."

"Have you spoken to any of the other known prostitutes in the area?" Holmes asked. "It would have been easy to target a woman walking alone—but perhaps one of her cohorts saw her, or noticed something amiss in her demeanor. Perhaps she was even feuding with a client or a lover."

"We have officers canvassing the neighborhood now," Grant answered. "So far, we've had multiple reports from those who noticed her in what would have been the last hours of her life. Though I must admit the residents of Whitechapel are not usually cooperative with our investigations, they seem to have come together when faced with this present horror. Everything we have uncovered so far will be in the file I shall give you to review."

"I have one final question," concluded Holmes. "I suppose Mary's body has been handled by a number of officers today, not to mention the coroner and his assistant?"

Grant looked confused, but nodded affirmation. "And I suppose the ambulance driver, as well—why do you ask?"

"I shall explain it more clearly later,"

answered Holmes. "There's a revolutionary new technique I have been experimenting with—it has to do with fingerprints, and capturing them from various surfaces, even human flesh. But with Mary I suppose it is much too late—if any of her clients' or her murderer's fingerprints remained upon her body, they have likely been smudged too much to be of any use."

After a little more discussion about the grisly crime itself, the coroner pulled the sheet back over Mary Ann's face and put the body back into the drawer. The detectives returned to Grant's office.

"Here is the file," Grant said as he handed it to Holmes. "There are several witnesses you will need to see and question. I trust you will get started right away, and report back to me anything you find. We want to nail this down as soon as we can, before panic takes hold of the city."

"Of course, sir."

"We have given you a desk to work from, should you prefer being here some days rather than in your own office on Baker Street. My secretary will show you—please don't hesitate to ask should you need anything. The entire force of Scotland Yard is at your disposal."

"Thank you very much," Holmes nodded.

"Wait," said Grant as Holmes turned to study the list. "You promised you would explain the importance of fingerprints—you know I am most interested in any new form of gathering evidence. Please take the time to share this knowledge with me."

"It's very simple," answered Holmes. "Hold your fingers up to your face and examine them."

He waited while Grant did so.

"You will notice the whorls and ridges on the pad of each finger—they are unique not only from finger to finger, but from man to man. A German anatomist discovered this in 1788, in fact. Fingerprints have been used to identify individuals, or to serve as their signatures, since even ancient Babylonian times, and in more recent times—less than a decade ago—a Scottish physician proposed using fingerprints as a means of identification."

Grant nodded, realization dawning across his face; he also looked a bit abashed. Holmes, suspecting why, continued on.

"This surgeon, Dr. Henry Faulds, even came to the Metropolitan police two years ago and offered the technique to Scotland Yard—

though they were not interested. It is a shame—a travesty, even—that the good men here did not listen to Dr. Faulds. When this technique is honed and refined, as it one day will be, it will serve as a fail-safe means of identifying who has touched an object, or even a body. I'm sure you can see how invaluable that would be to investigations and eliminating—or confirming—suspects."

Grant hung his head. "I remember the surgeon of whom you speak; and I will admit I dismissed him without much thought. I believed he was a crackpot, and we are so busy here. I am not a man of science, and I did not take time to listen to his theories."

"It is never too late to right a wrong," said Holmes. "And if we can get a fingerprint from the body or the belongings of the next victim, it may solve our case for us."

"Tell me what to do," said Grant. "I will ensure it is done."

"When—or rather if—there is another murder, instruct your officers to barricade off the area as quickly as possible; instruct them sternly to refrain from touching the body. Call me, and I will dust the body and the surroundings for fingerprints."

"Dust it?" said Grant. "Of course I will do

as you ask—but what do you mean by dusting it?"

"I have been experimenting, as I said," answered Holmes. "Dusting is a way of making the fingerprints visible, using a variety of substances and some very careful collection methods. So far I have had fairly reliable results with very finely sifted ashes, and I am still considering other ways of lifting a print."

"Fascinating," said Grant. "I will instruct the officers as you have requested."

The witness list Grant left him with was long. Holmes had his work cut out for him, and he knew he would not only need intelligence but also stamina to see this case through to its conclusion.

Holmes and the first witness, a man named Mr. Henry Birch, sat down at Birch's kitchen table. Mr. Birch was the proprietor of a milk stand near where the murder had occurred.

"At a little past eleven a man came to my stand, and said he quite desperately wanted a glass of milk. He appeared nervous, his eyes darting around, and he was carrying a black bag. I gave him the milk, which he drank down hurriedly, and then he asked if he might step into the yard beside my stand. I said I had no objection—and why should I have?—but I became suspicious upon reconsidering his demeanor. When I stepped out to check on him, I saw that he was pulling on a pair of overalls. The man paused and said, 'That was a terrible murder last night, wasn't it?' and then he picked up his bag and was gone," Birch continued. "I thought he might be a detective in disguise, or even an engineer once I saw the overalls."

"Did you recognize him?"

"No, sir. I had never seen the fellow before."

"Can you give me any details of his appearance?" Holmes asked.

"Well, he had on a blue suit with a stand-up collar, and a low hat, and a watch chain hanging from his pants. He had a slight mustache and his face seemed to be a little sunburned—perhaps he was even a sailor or some other sort of seafaring man. Say, do you think it was the killer himself?"

"I can't speak on the matter so early in the investigation," Holmes answered. "Though I'd appreciate any other detail you may remember."

That was all Mr. Birch could tell him, so Holmes excused himself to move on to the next witness. First, though, he would join forces with Dr. Watson—his friend always had some insight to add, and would be an invaluable ally in interviewing the remaining witnesses.

"Would it not be better to call the witnesses into Scotland Yard?" asked Dr. Watson. "If time is of the essence, such a strategy will save you a substantial amount of time."

"Jolly good idea, Watson. I knew I kept you around for some reason," Holmes laughed. "I suspect some witnesses would be more comfortable speaking in their own homes or place of work, but if I feel that's the case I can always make a personal follow-up visit later on."

Holmes proceeded to send messengers out to find and invite everyone on his list and set up appointments starting within the hour.

Holmes also sent a message to Mrs. Parker that both he and Dr. Watson would return to the house on Baker Street for a late supper; he didn't want the kindly maid to worry about them, and he also didn't want a cold meal after such a long day of work.

Before returning to the station, Holmes and Dr. Watson walked through the dank streets of Whitechapel, where they found a crowd of citizens indulging their nosiness and slinking around to steal a look at where the woman had been murdered. Police were still there cleaning up and trying to dispatch the onlookers. There was nothing useful left at the scene.

Holmes thought briefly to himself that he must request that Scotland Yard close off any future murder scene as quickly as possible—chances were they had lost valuable evidence by not doing so.

CHAPTER FOUR
Insights

Holmes and Watson sat in the small, cold interview room waiting for their first witness to arrive. It was Sarah Colwell.

"Hello, Mrs. Colwell. Thank you for coming in on such short notice," Holmes told her as she walked in and sat down.

"Oh, you are most welcome," the blonde matron answered. She was small, and appeared nervous—she wrung her hands as she sat down, and repeatedly smoothed her worn skirt. "I have children—I want this murderer caught as much as anyone. I want my little ones to be safe on the street."

"Of course you do, ma'am—that's exactly what we're trying to do, to make the streets safe. Now, what did you observe on the night of the murder?"

"I live only about 120 yards from where the murder occurred in Buck's Row. I heard what sounded like running, and someone shouting 'murder, police!' It sounded like the person was running from another person—though I admit I only heard one set of footsteps. Now, my children were the ones who woke me.

They said someone was trying to get in our front door and was screaming," Mrs. Colwell said. "From talking to my neighbors, they also heard someone screaming 'murder, police' about five or six times. This happened around midnight."

"And that's all you can tell us?"

"Yes it is. I hope it helps," answered the witness.

"Yes, it does. Thank you very much," Holmes said as he dismissed the woman.

"Her story doesn't sound like it will be of much use," Holmes told Dr. Watson after Mrs. Colville had left the room. "The murder took place at three-forty in the morning. Whatever Mrs. Colwell heard occurred far earlier—such a ruckus is likely even common-place in an area such as Buck's Row. And how could she possibly have concluded that the person screaming was running from another person if she only heard one set of footsteps?"

"You are quite right, old friend. Also, despite Mrs. Colwell's claims about the neighbors, no one else has come forward saying they heard any commotion—so the noise could be an earlier murder attempt that was thwarted," said Dr. Watson. "Or it could merely have been a drunk."

Next, the two men who had found the body, Charles Cross and Robert Paul, entered the room.

"Mr. Cross, how did you come to be at the site of the murder?"

"Well, I leave for work every morning around three-twenty, so I was passing by the alley about ten minutes later. I noticed what I thought was a tarpaulin laying on the ground. Out of curiosity, I walked over to see what it was, and discovered it was a person," the man said.

"That's when he called to me as I was walking down the street in the vicinity," chimed in Robert Paul. "I walked over to Mr. Cross and felt the woman's hand—it was quite cold, and I felt no pulse."

"You are sure you felt nothing?" Holmes asked.

"Well, almost positive. I thought she was most likely dead, especially when I noticed all the blood," he answered.

"Then what did you do?"

"We were both late for work, so we left."

"Did it not occur to either of you that you should have notified the police immediately?" Holmes questioned, squinting in irritation.

"Perhaps the perpetrator was still nearby!"

"Well, yes, we should have gone to the police right away," answered Robert Paul, "but we needed to get to our jobs. Work is not so easy to find, you know. We saw a policeman standing at the crossing of Hanbury Street and Baker's Row and told him what we had seen. He told us his name was Jonas Mizen, and that he would notify the police. We then went on our way."

The next witness to arrive was James Hatfield. He was an inmate in the Whitechapel workhouse, employed as a dock laborer. He had been brought to the morgue around 6:30 A.M. to help undress the victim in order for the doctor to make his examination; Donald Hamilton, who had been in charge of the morgue at that time, had accepted the body.

"Tell me about undressing the body," Holmes requested. "No detail is too small."

"I removed her overcoat and cut the bands of her petticoat to remove it; her dress I pulled down with my hands," Hatfield said very nervously. "She also had on a chemise, which I removed as well."

"Were you instructed not to touch the body?"

"I don't remember that," Hatfield said. "I undressed her, but I do not recall if I touched the body except to remove her clothes or not. My memory is not very good."

"Was she wearing stays?" Holmes asked.

"I do not recall. Mr. Hamilton said she was when we talked later, but I can't say I have any personal recollection."

This man's demeanor seemed a little suspicious to Holmes and Dr. Watson, but it was unlikely he had had anything do with the murder. He was just a pauper forced into the workhouse by London society, and there could have been many reasons why he acted so oddly. They still did not know if he had inadvertently ruined any evidence.

The next witness, Emily Holland, was a woman in the same profession as Mary. She was tall and thin, and seemed to be a little nervous and exhausted. She admitted to being a friend of Mary's and even stayed in the same lodging house at 18 Thrawl Street. Indeed, she was the person the police had called to positively identify Mary, so she had already been to the stationhouse once that day.

"I ran across Mary in the street after I returned from seeing a fire at the dry dock about 2:30 A.M., and I noticed that she was very drunk," Emily told them. "I was in the same shape and suggested that we go to my kitchen and sober up, but Mary refused."

"What did she say to you?"

"She told me how much money she had earned that night and also how much she had spent on drinks. She said she wished she could find a man to stay the night with," the woman said. "After a few minutes, we said 'goodnight' and parted ways. That was the last time I laid eyes on Mary."

"Did she mention anyone following her?" Holmes asked, thinking back on the woman who heard yelling and knocking on doors.

"No, not a word. She seemed fine to me...just drunk."

"Thank you for your help—we'll be in touch if we require anything further."

Emily's eyes began to water as she stood up, and Dr. Watson noticed she was trembling. "I hope you can find the monster who killed Mary soon," Emily said. "There's too many of us out there in the nighttime with no protection against such evil."

"We will do our best," Dr. Watson said. "That we can promise you."

Holmes got up to stretch his legs. "Would you like some tea, Doctor?" he asked.

"Yes, that would be splendid," Dr. Watson answered.

Holmes went over to the teapot and fetched two cups of steaming, hot tea. As he leaned over slightly to hand one to his friend, Watson heard a slight cracking sound.

"My back is so stiff," Holmes said. "This is not at all like sitting in my comfortable chair in my study."

"No, and we do not have dear Mrs. Parker to bring us coffee and sandwiches," answered Dr. Watson. "But we are doing important work, so I suppose stiff backs and growling stomachs are part and parcel of the experience."

"Sagacious as always," Holmes answered as he looked down at his witness list. Next on the list was Harriet Lilley; he called out for her to be sent in.

"Mrs. Lilley. Where do you live?" asked Holmes as he started another page in his notebook.

"I live at 7 Buck's Row, right across from where the murder took place," she said. "I happened to be sleeping in the front of the house and could hear everything that took place in the street. I heard a moan and a few faint gasps. On that street it is not uncommon to hear some of those sounds late at night—it gets to be so you don't think anything about them. I also heard what sounded like voices coming from right under my window," she continued. "I thought it may have been lovers having a meeting or prostitutes at work, so I rolled over and went back to sleep."

She shifted in her seat, apparently uncomfortable that she had not gotten up to look out her window.

"In the morning, I mentioned the disturbance to my husband and then we found out about the murder, so now I believe what I heard was a woman being attacked."

"So nothing aroused your suspicions at the time?"

"No, not until the morning. But now I realize the sounds were probably from someone in pain."

John Neil and John Thain were the two policemen who met Jonas Mizen at the scene of the crime. John Thain was a police constable and had arrived just in time to help load Mary's body into the ambulance. He noticed the back of her dress was drenched with blood and had even gotten some of it on his hands.

"It was dark, but I could tell the woman's

eyes were wide open. Blood was still oozing from the cuts on her throat," he said. "Her hat was lying alongside her body, and I noticed her arm was cold. I knew we had another murder and sent for an ambulance."

"Did you check for any witnesses?"

"Yes, I did check with workers at Essex Wharf to see if they had heard anything, but they claimed they had not. There were also a couple of men who worked at a nearby horse-slaughtering factory who came by to see what was going on. They had not seen or heard anything either."

"Is there anything else you can tell us?" asked Holmes.

"No. I stayed there until the ambulance took her away."

"Thank you for stopping by."

About that time, Inspector Grant arrived. "Are you getting anything useful?" he asked as he nodded to Dr. Watson.

"Not particularly. A few of the blanks have been filled in, but I can't say there have been any strong insights into the murder so far. I really haven't had the time to study over my notes though, so I may find something yet."

"We are still trying to locate more witnesses, but I think you have them all. Most people are nervous to come forward with the other murders going on. I am still not sure if those crimes are connected to this one."

"I will say it again: I tend to believe, from what I have read in the papers, that this murderer is different. It may even be the man's first murder, and I hope to God it will be his last, but unfortunately, another murder may be the only way we catch him," Holmes said.

"Well, keep up the good work and let me know of any resources that you need," Grant said as he walked away.

The next witness was John Spratling. He had arrived on the scene after the blood had been washed away by a neighbor boy and the victim was already in the ambulance. He and Sergeant George Godley were the investigators who checked with the surrounding neighbors to see if they could find any witnesses. There was not much to add there.

"What did you do after you helped load the victim?" asked Holmes.

"I searched the Great Eastern and East London railways, Essex Wharf, and the District Railway as far as Thomas Street for witnesses and clues. I did not have any luck."

That concluded the day's interviews.

CHAPTER FIVE
Profiled

The week was a whirlwind of activity. Holmes and Dr. Watson worked tirelessly to verify witnesses' stories, as well as to call in more people to give testimony—though most of it amounted to nothing. Poor Mary was buried, her mourners made up of people who lived in her lodging house or friends from the bar.

To Holmes' immense frustration, the investigation was going nowhere. He grew tenser and more taciturn than usual, but he was loath to admit the murder was linked to the others that had taken place. It was too violent and too bizarre—he knew in his gut that they were not connected. A week later, on the eighth of September, Holmes' initial reaction was confirmed: another body was found under much the same conditions as the first one.

Annie Chapman was a widow and the mother of three grown children who had long since moved on to live their own lives. She was short, about five feet four inches tall, with mousy blond hair; she was 47 years of age. Her husband had been dead for years, and she had never gotten back on her feet financially. John had died from cirrhosis of the liver and Annie, herself, was an alcoholic. It helped to deaden the pain of having no family around. At first, she had taken in needlework to make ends meet—when she still failed to earn enough to live, she turned to prostitution.

In September 1888, she lived in a lodging house where the boarders paid by the day. She had been down on her luck and did not have the money for even one more night. She told the landlord, as he kicked her out, that she would have the money when she returned; he did not believe her, although she begged him to hold her a room. He waved her off as she drunkenly left the house and stepped out into the streets of Spitalfields.

She would never need that room—for the next morning she was found murdered in the backyard of a house on Hanbury Street.

As soon as the police had been notified, Inspector Grant sent a messenger to Holmes and told him the address where the murder had taken place. Holmes immediately dressed and made his way to the scene, a notebook in his breast pocket. Dr. Watson did not come with him this time, being otherwise committed.

The poor woman lay there with two deep cuts on her throat, both of which reached her spine—exactly as Mary had been mutilated. Annie's stomach had been ripped wide open and her uterus, upper vagina, and two thirds of her bladder were missing. All of her small intestines had been chopped and removed but remained behind, laid out upon her right shoulder. Portions of her pubic area had been put on her left shoulder. It was a horrid sight, and Holmes had to fight himself not to retch. The officers at the scene were pale and shocked, and the mood was a somber one.

"I guess this confirms it, Detective," Holmes told Grant. "We have a serial killer now. These two murders are nothing like the other ones."

"Yes, I am afraid you are right, dear Sherlock. The town will go wild when they know we have a monster in our midst," Grant said. "We will have to post bulletins warning the women in this area—they must stay off the streets. Though I doubt many listen, as they rely heavily on any small daily income they make."

"Did the officers touch the victim's clothing?" Holmes asked. "Has anyone, to your knowledge, touched the body?"

"My officers swear they have not," said Grant.

"Come with me, then," said Holmes.

He and Grant knelt by the body, and Holmes took a small, soft brush from his pocket, along with a packet of dark powder.

"Graphite," he said by way of explanation. "Though I have been thinking further about fingerprinting, and I doubt we would be able to get any from the body itself; any sweat, hair, or violent movement would interfere with a clear impression."

"Will you dust all of her?" said Grant, looking worried. "That seems indecorous. We must respect the dead."

"I will just dust the places where the Ripper might have seized her," answered Holmes. "Her wrists, or her neck. Of course, if she was wearing a brooch or other piece of jewelry on which a fingerprint would show clearly, that would be ideal."

Grant watched as Holmes methodically went about dusting the body, and a short time later the detective rose to his feet. "Nothing—this time," he said. "But perhaps we will still gather important evidence from any witnesses who were nearby."

"My officers are preparing a list according

to the usual protocol," said Grant. "Is there anything else we should know?"

"I have been thinking in depth upon this, yes," said Holmes. "I suspect this killer has advanced knowledge of human anatomy—a layperson could not have so efficiently removed the missing organs, or even identified them in the carnage. Our perpetrator could be a doctor, a butcher, a medical student, and there are even more possibilities beyond that."

"Yes, I thought of that too—that he must have some sort of specialized education or skill. He quite possibly lives in the area too, since these identical murders are less than a mile apart."

"Perhaps," said Holmes. "Though he would be a bold and reckless killer to make his hunting grounds anywhere near his own home."

Annie's body was removed, and Holmes remained at the scene until he was sure he had left no clue behind; it was still quite early in the morning. He then went home to pick up Dr. Watson, for he knew his friend would be there waiting on him. Then they would go to Scotland Yard and work up a profile—it was finally time to employ a technique taught to him by his old friend, Edmond Dantes.

As Holmes waited for Dr. Watson to finish the breakfast Mrs. Parker had prepared for them, Sherlock began to look through several days' worth of mail; though he was a tidy man, it often slipped his mind to sort it. When a postcard slipped from the mix, Holmes reached down to his feet to retrieve it—*how odd*, he thought. *None of my acquaintances have gone abroad or on any sort of trip.* The postcard had a picture of a bubbling brook on the front. Scrawled on the card were the words, *"The game has begun."*

A flash of confusion jolted through him. Who would send him such a cryptic message? Was this from the killer? Had he zeroed in on Holmes as a contact? It was not news that Holmes was working on the cases with the police—he was a prominent figure in London after so many successful investigations in the past—so it would have been quite simple to find out his address. There was no postmark, so someone had dropped the card directly into his mail slot. Holmes was intimidated by no man, but he was irritated that anyone would dare to disturb the privacy and comfort of his home, even with something as small as a postcard.

"Look, Watson," he said to his friend.

After Dr. Watson had read the card, he looked puzzled. "Do you believe this is from the killer? Could he be targeting you?"

"I can't think of who else would send me such an obscure message—and any friends or acquaintances would know I would not be amused by any sort of riddle or game."

"Oh, Holmes. That worries me so. We have to find this killer before he does anything to you."

"I don't believe he wants to hurt me—we mustn't jump to that conclusion. I think he knows of my skill as an investigator and is daring me to catch him. It probably amuses him to taunt me as he waits to find his next victim. Let's be off to the Yard and get to work on that profile."

"Immediately, of course," Dr. Watson said, pushing himself away from the table.

"Also, let's not mention this card to Inspector Grant for the time being. I want to decide what to do on my own," Holmes told his friend.

"Rightly so. It is your business, after all, and I can't see how Inspector Grant knowing of the message would help him solve the crime."

Once Holmes reached his desk at Scotland Yard, he pulled out his notebook and pen and started jotting down thoughts as they came into his head. The great Count of Monte Cristo had taught him a few things about a method of investigation called criminal profiling, and he intended to finally put this knowledge to use. He wished his dear friend could be with him now—he was sure the Count would have some insight even the great Sherlock Holmes couldn't deduce on his own.

"Watson, I do not believe this person is married. If he ever was, it was most likely to a woman much older, and the union failed a short time after it was started."

Dr. Watson furrowed his brow. "And how have you concluded this?" he asked. "I'm not sure I follow your reasoning."

"Both of the victims have been women in middle age," Holmes answered. "There are legions of young, beautiful women on the streets as well—and yet our murderer is targeting victims of a certain age. I also believe that most of his sexual encounters have been with prostitutes. He seems to be focusing himself on them. He may even be impotent, since no violations occur either before or after the murder."

"That is very interesting," said Dr. Watson. "What else have you come upon?"

"I think that the clothes he wears are not his everyday attire. To approach a prostitute, he would need to look as if he has the money, and thus he dresses in his finest—if he appears wealthy, the women would be much more likely to go with him into a dark alley, in hopes that he would pay well for their services. I also feel he is a loner; otherwise, someone would notice the odd hours he must keep, not to mention any clothing covered in blood."

"Well, what about his job? How can he be up all night to do these murders and still report regularly to work?"

"As I mentioned before, I believe he has to know the human anatomy to a certain degree. He could have a job where he works mostly alone," Holmes continued. "He would be able to keep his own hours, or have some flexibility in them. Or perhaps he just doesn't require much sleep. There have been two murders, with one week in between—one sleepless night a week would not affect a healthy, strong man in any real way. And he may not have a job at all."

Inspector Grant walked up at that time.

"Have you had any luck in your profiling?" he asked as he pulled up a chair. "I can't say I've ever heard of your method, but I trust it will yield something of value to our investigation."

"We are just getting started," Holmes told him. "It is an involved process, and one that takes much concentration and thought."

He passed over his notes and let Grant read what he had just written.

Holmes lit a cigar, took a long drag, and continued. "I think this man holds things inside and they come out in his doing destructive, awful things. Murder is the only way he can get relief from his inner demons."

"So murdering these women is a way to vent his own frustration and anger?" Grant asked.

"Yes. I fear there will be more murders. He appears to just be getting started, given the distinctive signature he is leaving on each body. Maybe those other murders in the area gave him the impetus to get started, but I do not know."

"What else do you suspect?" Grant inquired. "I will eagerly listen to any theory you have."

"I do think he lives in the Whitechapel

area, as you yourself suggested, and he could have some kind of physical deformity or other strange characteristic that makes him uncomfortable around people. That could also be why he strikes in the dark, where he can move with confidence."

"Yes."

"I also believe he is quiet and unassuming. Nobody would ever take a second look at this person. He may even have been interrogated as a witness already. We should undertake some door-to-door questioning of people living in the area of the murders, in case we missed a witness in our first sweep. Chances are, he will be one of those we speak to."

Inspector Grant thought for a minute. "Please make a list of your thoughts that we can post for all the detectives to see. Keep working on your profile, but make haste with it. I also fear he is not done, and we need to work swiftly," Grant told Holmes.

Dr. Watson wrote out the list, since he had impeccable handwriting, and it was posted for the detectives to see. Each patrolman had his own copy as well.

Jack the Ripper

CHAPTER SIX
Taunting Card

The next day, Holmes and Watson went out into the field to conduct interviews about Annie's murder. There weren't as many witnesses as there had been with Mary's murder, but Holmes still held out hope that they would discover something substantial.

Their first stop was to the Crossingham's Lodging House on Dorset Street, the place where Annie lived when she could afford it. The cost was eight pence a night for a bed. They had made an appointment to speak to the landlord, Timothy Donovan, about his tenant.

"Mr. Donovan, can you tell us about the night before Annie was found murdered and anything else you remember about her?"

"Yes sir. Annie had a terrible time keeping her rent paid. She drank the money away most times and I could not keep giving her a room for free, so some nights I had to turn her away. This was the case on that night," the landlord told them.

"What do you mean?" asked Dr. Watson.

"Well, she had not been feeling well and

had come to the last of her money. She asked if she could sit in the kitchen with her friends for a while that night. I told her she could. She was a nice woman and did embroidery and sold flowers to supplement her income. I knew she had fallen on some hard times, but I can't just give away my rooms. I have to make money too," the man said, feeling a sharp pang of guilt for sending Annie into the night alone.

"Please continue."

"She had two regular clients—a man named Harry, though I can't remember his surname, and Ted Stanley. Ted visited here often and would pay me to turn her out if she had any liaisons with another. He will deny this and say he only visited her once or twice, I would bet, but trust me, he was a regular. I can give you his address if you want. He doesn't live far from here, but I have to tell you he is married. If you do visit him, I'm sure he would appreciate discretion."

"We will collect the address from you at the end of our talk," said Holmes. "Do you have any other details you want to discuss with us?"

"Eliza Cooper is another guest here frequently, and she and Annie used to be friends, but they had a bad argument recently. She resides in room number three, and may be able to give you more details about Annie's life than I can."

"Thank you again."

The men finished up their interview and asked to see Eliza, but were told she was out, so they decided to go visit Mr. Stanley and then come back. He said exactly what the landlord had said he would say, and upon conclusion of that interview they returned to Dorset Street to speak with Eliza.

"Ms. Cooper, we understand that you and the murder victim had an argument not long before her death," Holmes told the woman seated in front of him at the kitchen table of the lodging house.

"Well, she borrowed some soap from me and never returned it. She let one of her men use it, and every time I asked for it back, she gave me some excuse. Money doesn't grow on trees you know," the woman said with a sneer. "I can't be buying soap willy-nilly."

"Of course—we do understand that. We also understand that you saw Annie in a bar and slapped her, which started an argument. Annie's body had bruises on it, and they seem to be from you hitting her."

"She had it coming. She threw a penny at me and told me to go buy a penny's worth of soap!"

"That does not sound like cause for a fistfight," Holmes told her.

"Maybe not—but I've always had a fierce temper. I am sorry she is dead. We used to be friends," the woman said, growing pensive. "Are we safe here?"

"We are doing our best to make it so."

Continuing, she said, "I do remember seeing Annie on Hanbury Street that morning about 5:30. She was talking to a man whose back was to me. The man said 'Will you?' and she said, 'Yes.' That's all I heard. He was not dressed very sharply, so he probably did not have money, and those sorts of men do not interest me."

"We are doing everything we can to catch the killer. If you have any other information you can give us we would appreciate it," Holmes said as he took out a few business cards and gave them to her. "If you would pass that along to the other tenants, we would appreciate it."

With that, the two men took their leave and went to see Albert Cadosh, who lived next door to where Annie's body had been found.

"What can you tell us, sir, about this morning?" Holmes asked the man who answered their knock at the door and identified himself as Mr. Cadosh.

"It was about 5:30 A.M. when I went into the backyard of my house. I heard a woman's voice say 'no.' That's all. I was too busy relieving my bladder to snoop. But when my neighbor, John Davis, went into his back yard at number twenty-nine about 6:00 A.M. and discovered the body, I knew it had to be the woman I had heard."

"Did you wait for the police and ambulance to come and get the body?"

"Yes, I did."

"Have you been interrogated by any other police about this?"

The man told them he had, so Holmes and Dr. Watson knew they probably would not have much to add to this man's file.

They found Amelia Palmer, their next witness, at the corner bar. When they announced who they were and asked for anyone to step forward if they had seen Annie that morning, Ms. Palmer walked over to them.

"Annie was my friend. I saw her just a few days before on the street. She had bruising on her right temple and looked very upset. She also opened up her dress and showed me bruising on her chest. She told me she had gotten into a fight with a woman at the tavern. I was real worried about her, because she had not been feeling well lately." The woman fingered the buttons running down the front of her dress. "I also saw her a couple of days later. She looked no better, and I asked if she had eaten. She told me she had not, and that she had been feeling poorly, so I gave her a little money and told her not to spend it on drink. I don't know if she did or not."

"Do you have reason to believe she was in danger?"

"I do not know, but I did pass her just yesterday, standing on the street corner with a man. She made some remark that she 'couldn't give it away, she had to make some money or she wouldn't have a place to stay.' Those were the last words I heard from her."

"Do you recall what the fellow looked like?" asked Holmes.

Amelia closed her eyes for a moment, trying to remember the scene. "I think he was dark complected—I wasn't paying much attention to his face, to be honest—but I do know he was wearing a leather apron. I thought that was very odd—of course, butchers and even surgeons wear them—but they usually don't wander the streets in them."

Holmes got a gleam in his eye at this time—one of his suspicions had been confirmed—but he said nothing further other than to thank Amelia for her time.

Dr. Watson had to return home, and Holmes walked to the station to rewrite his notes and compare them with any others taken from these witnesses. Inspector Grant, seeing the detective had returned, hurried over to his desk.

"Holmes, I need to speak with you."

"Yes sir."

With that, Grant tossed one of Holmes' business cards on the desk before him.

"Where did you get my card?" questioned Holmes.

"It was found part-ways under the body of our latest murder victim," Grant answered.

There was a stunned silence.

"I do not understand," Holmes said.

"Could you have dropped your card during the examination of Annie's body?" asked Grant.

"I suppose it's possible." But Holmes was thinking that he did not have any business cards with him that morning. He had taken a fresh suit and only put his cards into the pocket when he and Dr. Watson returned home. He did not reveal this little fact—his instincts told him to keep it as quiet as he had the message he received in the mail. He would discuss it with Dr. Watson later that evening. He was sure now that the killer was taunting him.

"Well, I thought that's probably what happened. I just wanted to let you know. Keep up the good work, Holmes."

With that, Inspector Grant was on his way.

More witnesses came in and out during the rest of the day, but Holmes was not involved in all of the interviews. His mind was only half-heartedly operating at that time. The question that kept running through his thoughts was, *Why is this killer targeting* me?

CHAPTER SEVEN
In So Many Words

Mrs. Parker prepared a fine supper that night. She had roasted a pig and sautéed new potatoes in garlic and butter with asparagus and cheese sauce. The bread was crusty and fresh, and the ale was chilled. The men's mouths were watering just walking to the table. They were both famished, and they felt at that moment an immense appreciation for Mrs. Parker.

Holmes told his friend about the day's events and asked for his advice.

"It does seem that our culprit is bringing you into this, Holmes. You have to be very careful, or else you will be accused of these murders before you know it," Dr. Watson told him. "Especially if the police find another of your cards at a murder scene."

"How well I know this—though I would like to believe that Scotland Yard would be clever enough to realize a murderer would not leave his own name at the scene of every crime. Do you think I did the right thing by holding my tongue about the postcard and what I know about the business card? Should I tell Grant?"

"No, I think you are doing the right thing at this point. We have to find out how the murderer got your card. Do you have any ideas?"

"No."

"Well, I imagine there are any number of your cards circulating London—you leave them when you make a call, or investigate witnesses. Perhaps you have given out your card to the murderer without knowing it."

"True. Both could be true. We will just see what happens next and be on the alert. I will need you to help me, old friend, by searching any future murder sites. If this vile fellow is trying to frame me, he's not as clever as I thought—or otherwise he would not use so obvious a method. I think he is merely trying to catch my attention and let me know that he is very aware I am on his trail."

The men stayed up most of the night going over the interviews from both murders. There did not seem to be a common thread among them as far as identifying a perpetrator. The only connection between the murders was that the way the killing was performed was almost identical; that the victims were prostitutes; and that the victims were of a similar age. Holmes and Watson needed to concentrate on the profile and pay close attention when they did their interviews as to whom among the suspects had the traits they had identified.

The next day at the precinct, a loud buzz of excited conversation blanketed the room. The mail had just run. A letter had arrived that was supposedly from the murderer. Everyone was called together and the letter read.

Dear Boss,

I keep on hearing the police have caught me but they won't fix me just yet. I have laughed when they look so clever and talk about being on the right track. That joke about Leather Apron gave me real fits. I am down on whores and I shan't quit ripping them till I do get buckled. Grand work in the last job was. I gave the lady no time to squeal. How can they catch me now. I love my work and want to start again. You will soon hear of me with my funny little games. I saved some of the proper red stuff in a ginger beer bottle over the last job to write with but it went thick like glue and I can't use it. Red ink is fit enough I hope ha. Ha. The next job I do I shall clip the lady's ears off and send to the police officers just for jolly wouldn't you. Keep this letter back till I do a bit more work, then give it out straight. My knife's so nice and sharp I want to get to work right away if I get a chance. Good luck.

Yours truly,
Jack the Ripper

Don't mind me giving the trade name.

P.S. Wasn't good enough to post this before I got all the red ink off my hands curse it. No luck yet. They say I'm a doctor now. Haha

Silence. Everyone was deep in thought, and then the noise of chatter and speculation became deafening once more.

"Now everyone, we must focus," Inspector Grant said. "Go by the profile Inspector Holmes wrote for us. Pay close attention to anyone you run across, no matter how mild-mannered or innocent they seem. Remember, this man more than likely looks just like an everyday citizen. He's told us he's planning another murder, so we must be swift and try to stay ahead of the game."

Holmes stepped forward and gestured for the men to wait just as they started to disperse. "Sirs, please give me a moment more of your day. When you're studying the profile and interviewing witnesses, you must keep one thing in the forefront of your mind: logic. There's nothing more important in solving crimes.

"Though many cultures have had famed fathers of logical thinking, in England we are most familiar with the Greek philosopher Aristotle. There are many forms of logic, but the basis he gave us—which evolved into a focus on inductive and deductive reasoning—remains the most important for investigatory work in today's era.

"Inductive reasoning is the process of drawing a conclusion from a set of observations—but this process only works if there is absolutely no scenario in which the premises you've proposed are true and the conclusion is still false. Inductive reasoning gives weight to probabilities but not certainties; however, it can still be a useful tool for explaining all angles of a situation, though it should not be your primary tool.

"Deductive reasoning—there is the key! It gives us something a bit more concrete and reliable with which to work. With deductive reasoning, A invariably leads to B.

"I have said it to other audiences before, but it bears repeating—deduction is reasoning backwards. Take the conclusion, and all the data at hand, and try to go back—step by step. Don't theorize before you have all of the evidence—look at the conclusion without bias. Observe, but do not judge; keep your mind free of emotion, for it clouds your thoughts.

"If you can notice even the smallest, most insignificant detail—you may realize that it is not so insignificant at all, and may lead to a groundbreaking discovery.

"In sum, deductive reasoning helps you eliminate everything but the truth. While this thought process takes time to develop, it will be of immense value to you—and even I was once as new to it as you are."

Holmes stopped speaking abruptly and turned away to go about his day; he was thinking of the great man who had taught him the intricacies of logic: Edmond Dantes. The officers likewise returned to their duties, but Holmes' impassioned advice would stay with them for the rest of their careers, and it improved the work of many a Scotland Yard detective.

The streets of Whitechapel remained quiet for the next few days, and no new clues came to light. Everyone went about their daily routine of interviewing witnesses and comparing notes. The officers in Scotland Yard even thought the first letter was a hoax and that the murders had ended, but their hopes would soon be dashed. The precinct received a postcard in the mail. It read:

I was not codding dear old Boss when I gave you the tip, you'll hear about Saucy Jacky's work in the news tomorrow—double event this time number one squealed a bit couldn't finish straight off. Ha not the time to get ears for police. Thanks for keeping last letter back till I got to.

Jack the Ripper again

The letter was posted and distributed. All of the officers were on the alert that they might find another murder victim at any time. Holmes *knew* there would be at least one more victim. He had to stay on his toes to see if the murderer planted any more clues that would lead to his capture. Holmes wondered to himself why the fiend was committing such crimes, and whether perhaps he had met the maniac before.

Holmes went back over to the morgue to ask the coroner's assistant a few more questions. Donald was welcoming and friendly, and he led Holmes into a back room for privacy.

"Mr. Hamilton," Holmes started. "We've met before—how good to see you again. How many people have been in to view the body?"

"Well, right off the top of my mind I cannot tell you, but I will have a look at the log," Donald said. He left the room and returned a few moments with a leather-bound book.

"Let's see. You, of course, Inspector Grant, Inspector Jones..."

"Here, let me look please."

"Of course."

Holmes noticed that a few of Annie's friends had come and identified the body early on. Other than that, nobody else had viewed the victim other than those involved in the investigation.

"Thank you, Mr. Hamilton."

"You're welcome. Is there anything else I can help you with?"

"Not at this time—I merely wanted to see if any of the names jumped out at me as a potential murderer. If the Ripper could possibly get away with it, I think he would be amused at viewing the body of his victim so close to Scotland Yard, and yet walking away. And I must inquire, for the satisfaction of my own curiosity, how do you work around all of these dead people day in and day out?" Holmes asked.

"I guess you just get used to it. They are all people. These just don't carry on a conversation," Donald said, trying to lighten the moment.

"I do not believe I could do it," Holmes answered him.

"Well, we are each suited for our jobs. You find the criminals to keep our streets safe, and I help prepare those who have left this earth before they go to their final resting place."

"Yes, that is a good way to look at it," Holmes said, and then he thanked the assistant again and walked back to his desk in the precinct.

Two questions whirled in his brain: *What had he missed? When was the next murder coming?* Holmes had a suspicion that the Ripper's next act might be a double murder from the wording in the letter. He hoped he was wrong.

Jack the Ripper

CHAPTER EIGHT
Double Cut

Louis Diemshutz was a salesman of cheap jewelry. He was on his way home at about 1:00 A.M. in his horse-drawn cart. As the horse trotted into the alley connected to his back yard, the beast jolted to the left and almost turned over the cart.

"You silly horse," Louis scolded. "What a mess you almost made!"

The man glanced over and noticed a bundle lying on the ground. Louis got down off the cart and lit a match as he leaned over for a better look. A puff of wind quickly cast him back into darkness, but he got a quick peek and noticed the figure was that of a woman. He actually thought it was his wife, who had the occasional habit of getting drunk and passing out wherever she was. He took the horse and cart on to the shed. After the horse was curried and fed, he walked back over to where he thought his wife was sound asleep. On the way, he saw his wife through the kitchen window. He went inside.

"There is a woman lying in our back yard,

Molly. I thought it was you. Come with me to check on her," Diemshutz said to his surprised wife.

They both walked out with candles and saw that the woman was not merely passed out—she was dead. Her throat was cut down to her spine, and blood pooled on the ground beneath her. The shaken couple went to their neighbor's house and sent for the police.

Holmes was still awake, reading his notes, when a messenger knocked at his door and gave him directions to the new murder scene. He hurriedly dressed and caught a carriage to the destination, not knowing any details.

The scene was bustling with police by the time he arrived. Grant came up to Holmes and filled him in quickly on the situation. Dr. Llewellyn was there, bending down by the body. Holmes walked up to him and grabbed the man's wrist before he could touch the dead woman.

"Wait," Holmes said abruptly. "I suppose you won't be the first one to touch the body?"

The coroner looked confused. "Hello, Inspector. No, both the man who found her and several policeman have probably had some contact with the victim by now—why do you ask?"

Holmes sighed—it was enough to drive a man to swear. He would never get useable fingerprints at this rate. "No matter, sir. I will speak to Inspector Grant about it later. Tell me, is there anything different about this victim, in your opinion?"

"Well, this one is a little strange. I do believe the murderer was interrupted before he was completely finished. The only mark on the body is her throat being cut from the left side. Only one cut...on the other victims there were two," the coroner said. "There are no organs removed either. I think that when Diemshutz came into the yard with his cart, the culprit was still here and spooked the horse—Diemshutz said the horse almost overturned the cart. The murderer was probably hiding in the bushes. Had Diemshutz and his wife alerted the police at that moment, we may have found the fellow in the vicinity."

"That would have been a great feat to accomplish. But as it is, he had opportunity enough to escape, as the witness put up his horse and fetched his wife first. That probably took a fair amount of time," Holmes said thoughtfully.

Holmes searched the bushes to see if he

could find any sign of where the killer had hidden. There were several places where the grass was tamped down, and Holmes knew the thickness of it had probably muffled the sound of footsteps retreating. The murderer could so easily have been seen if it had not been dark! *Drat! This could have been the end of it,* he thought.

Holmes caught an officer and had him go around and take the names of everyone at the scene and the neighbors for a list of witnesses. Holmes would go over the list at the precinct and arrange for the witnesses he needed to come in for an interview. He stayed alert for any item or clue that could have been associated with himself, in case the killer had left something to tie him to the crime. This time, though, it appeared The Ripper was in such a hurry that he did not have time to plant false evidence.

About the time the body was being loaded into the cart that would take it to the morgue, a ripple of disturbance and intense whispering swept through the crowd. Holmes noticed his friend Dr. Watson walking toward him at a brisk pace.

"What has happened?" Holmes asked him.

"There has been another murder in Mitre

Square, London City."

"What?" Holmes asked in surprise. "Another, so soon?"

"Are you finished here?" Dr. Watson asked.

"Yes, for the time being. They are taking the body now to the morgue. We will go there later, but now we must go to the new scene," Holmes told Dr. Watson as he motioned to Inspector Grant and told him of his plans.

"I have brought my horse and carriage, so we can be on our way," Dr. Watson told Holmes.

They arrived on scene about 2:30 A.M. The place was already full of police from London City. Holmes and Dr. Watson found out the woman had been dead for only half an hour. That meant the killer had come there straightaway and committed the murder— perhaps he had been frustrated at not being able to properly finish up the last one.

The victim was Catherine Eddowes, forty-three years of age. Jack the Ripper's signature cut was there, through the throat to the spine, and her abdomen had been cut open. Part of her large intestine had been draped over her left shoulder and another piece had been cut and placed under her right arm as if for some sort of decoration. Her arms were outstretched and one leg bent. Her left kidney and part of her uterus had been removed. Something different had been done to this victim, though. Her face had cuts and bruises on it; her eyelids were cut through. There was no blood below the middle of the body, although an ungodly amount from the waist up. Her left earlobe had been cut off. There was no blood on the front of her clothes, but there were buttons scattered everywhere in the blood that surrounded her shoulders.

Holmes bent down as he saw something glinting through the blood; the item was caught in the glare of the gaslights. He picked it up with a handkerchief. Nobody was around except Dr. Watson as he looked at the item. By jove! It was his cigar cutter, engraved with SH!

"But how?" Dr. Watson started.

"Shhhh," Holmes said as he discreetly slipped the handkerchief into his coat pocket. Nobody was the wiser. Holmes broke out in a cold sweat—he had lost his cool, collected manner.

Someone came running up, saying they had found the woman's apron on the street not far from the scene of the killing. It had something scrawled on it:

"The Juwes are the men that will not be blamed for nothing."

Holmes asked the lead detective for that district to have a witness list sent over to him when they had it, and the detective assured him they would. Then Holmes told the officers he was going to the morgue.

Once they were safely in the carriage, Holmes removed the cigar cutter from his pocket once more and held it in his hands, his mouth set in a straight line.

"I do think leaving the business card was just to get my attention," Holmes said grimly. "And perhaps even to connect me to the crimes in Inspector Grant's mind. This cigar cutter, though—it means the fellow has been in my house, and has been watching both Mrs. Parker and I to ensure he won't get caught. If one more thing is found like this at the crime scene, I may find myself behind bars."

Dr. Watson felt a flutter of panic, but kept his voice calm for his friend's sake. "You have faced grave danger before, sir," he said. "This time is no different—and no one could ever believe you to be a murderer! We will catch this monster before he strikes again, and you will be able to rest easy."

"We must catch him," said Holmes. "Who knows what he will leave at the next scene—and more frightening, who knows who will find it first."

CHAPTER NINE
Brutality Rising

Upon arriving at the morgue, Holmes and Dr. Watson were met once again by Donald Hamilton.

"I didn't expect to see you here so early, Mr. Hamilton."

"Well, I haven't been here long. John Brooks is the other assistant, and we work twelve-hour shifts and swing our hours sometimes. His daughter is getting married today, and I agreed to cover for him."

"Well, it looks like you got stuck with the worst of it from these two murders. You will have another body coming fairly soon. They are almost done at the crime scene," Holmes warned him.

"Yes, I've heard. I guess you will want to see Elizabeth Stride, the first victim. Sign the log and we will proceed. I have been collecting evidence and getting her ready for my boss to perform the autopsy. He may even have to hire additional help if this keeps on. We seem to have had a full house lately."

Holmes liked Donald. Anyone who could keep his chin up in a place like this and maintain a pleasant demeanor even in the face of gruesome death was a special sort of man.

It did not take long to examine Elizabeth's body. The deed had obviously not been finished, and there seemed to be no other clues. As for now, there was nothing else that could be done.

As Holmes and Dr. Watson were preparing to leave, the police delivered the body of the latest victim. Holmes asked the coroner to send him a report as soon as he could, and they took their leave. He would get to work on the partial witness list that he had and familiarize himself with the women's histories.

Elizabeth, called Liz by her friends, was not known to be a full-time prostitute. She made money in a variety of other ways, including doing housework or sewing. She was also known to drink heavily and could get quite rowdy.

When she left the boarding house on the evening of her death, she had a little money from cleaning. Off into oblivion she went— which Holmes noted seemed to be a pattern with the victims. A drunk woman was less likely to be alert and would prove much easier to overcome than a woman in complete charge of her faculties.

The investigation also revealed that many people had seen Liz before her death. As

Constable William Smith was walking his beat that night, he saw Liz talking to a man around 12:30 A.M. He said the man was about thirty years old, very short—about five foot five inches tall—and had dark features. He was dressed in a dark coat, with a deerstalker hat on. He had a package in his hands.

Another witness, Israel Schwartz, saw a man talking to a woman about 12:45 A.M. The man shoved the woman into the street and she cried out softly three times. Schwartz did not see that the woman was in any immediate danger, and, thinking it was only a domestic dispute, he walked on. He did, however, notice another man of about thirty-five years old and height around five feet eleven inches, who was standing and watching the woman while smoking a pipe. Schwartz also noticed that the other man called out to the man with the pipe. *Perhaps there is even a pair of killers*, Holmes thought. *It is something to consider.*

William Marshall had been standing near the murder site about 11:45 P.M. He said that he had also seen Liz talking to a middle-aged man wearing what he called a "sailor" hat. The man looked to be about five feet six inches tall, was a little stout, and spoke like an educated man. It might not have been the murderer, since the conversation occurred almost an hour before the crime, but Holmes wouldn't rule it out.

James Brown was another witness who had seen Liz talking to a man of about five feet seven inches in a dark, long overcoat, minutes before her death. He heard Liz tell the man "not tonight, some other night."

These three witnesses had described someone who might have been the same man, Holmes thought, if you put all of their accounts together.

Holmes turned to the task of reading about and interviewing witnesses for Catherine's murder.

Catherine, until she was twenty-one years old, lived with her aunt because her mother and father had died. She did not appear to be a prostitute like the others, but one could not be sure of this if times were tough—perhaps she had just recently turned to the streets to make a living.

Holmes discovered from police records that Catherine had spent the night before in the police station. Officers had found her in a drunken stupor, propped up against a fence. The officers put her in a cell to sober up. She was so intoxicated that she did not even know her own name.

She woke up and was released at 1:00 A.M. on September 30 and was last seen walking in the direction of Mitre Square at the same time the murderer would have been traveling to the same destination.

Holmes had a note that Joseph Lawende, a cigarette salesman, had seen Catherine and a man talking on the street about 1:35 A.M., just ten minutes before her murder. Lawende said the man looked to be about thirty years old and stood about five foot seven inches tall; he had a mustache, a fair complexion, and a more or less average build. He was dressed like a sailor with a gray jacket and a red handkerchief tied around his neck. Lawende had said Catherine seemed relaxed, and perhaps had been familiar with the man.

Holmes had not eaten any breakfast, so he went over to a table where food and coffee and tea had been set up for all to enjoy. He had already helped himself to a sausage and a steaming cup of tea when Inspector Grant walked up.

"We are going to release the letter and post card today," Grant told Holmes. "The public has the right to know what we are up against so they can try to protect themselves. Perhaps if people see this is indeed a serial killer, they will be more cautious as they go about their lives."

"I agree, sir."

"Have you started to work on your witness lists yet?"

"Yes, but they are not complete. The remaining information should be brought in soon. I am looking over the coroner's report, but it may not tell us any more than we already know."

"Well, delegate your work. We are all in this together."

"Thank you, sir."

Holmes went back to his desk and found Dr. Watson waiting there for him, sipping a cup of tea.

"Hello, old friend," Holmes said. "The case is turning out to be trickier—and more personal—than I'd like. We must put an end to these murders, if only to keep from getting wrapped up in them ourselves."

The coroner's report for Catherine had appeared on Holmes' desk, and they read it slowly, trying to absorb the information fully and connect it to anything else they knew.

As the coroner had undressed and cleaned

the body, a piece of the deceased's ear had dropped from her clothes. This was something new. The body had even still been warm when it had arrived to the mortuary for the examination.

There had been many bruises on the body. Some had been old, but some were recent. The face was particularly mutilated, cut viciously. The left eyelid was severed almost all the way through. The nose was almost cut off. The cheeks had been cut and peeled up. The throat was cut across about seven inches. The liver had been cut as well. The larynx had been cut to the bone. The carotid artery had been cut, and Catherine had bled out fast. It seemed that the killer's rage was growing with every murder—or perhaps he had been taking out his frustration on not being able to properly mutilate the body of Liz.

All of the cuts to Catherine's body had been done after her death, and the perpetrator had used a very sharp knife, estimated to be six inches long. She had also been split from her vagina to the rectum. Considering the cuts, there would not have been that much blood to get on the murderer, as the attack had taken place from below the waist. The slashed throat would have prevented her from screaming, and it seemed to have occurred once she was already on the ground. There appeared to have been no struggle according to the officers who found the body, and there was no money on Catherine's person.

Holmes kept reading and was shocked at the brutality of it all. However, the specific mutilations done to the body re-confirmed for him that the murderer must have had some sort of medical training.

"Why do you think this one was so brutal?" asked Dr. Watson.

"I'm a few steps ahead of you there, old friend," answered Holmes. "I think it is because the murderer could not finish with the first victim to his satisfaction. Not much was done to her before he was interrupted. Of course, there was reference to a double homicide in the letter, so he had planned on two anyway."

"Have you been able to interrogate many witnesses yet?"

"No, but I see here I have two lists and should get to work. I am glad you're here to help me sort through this. The other detectives have been hard at work too, and have left me their notes."

The first witness, George Clapp, lived in a

house that was right next to where the murder occurred. He and his wife and a nurse for his wife were sleeping with their windows open that night and had heard nothing.

John Kelly, Liz's suitor, was called in to speak with Holmes.

"Did you know the victim well?" asked Holmes.

"Yes sir. We lived together. She was a good woman although she liked to drink. She had told me the day before her murder that she was going to visit her daughter and would be back in the late afternoon," Kelly told him. His face was pale with sorrow, and his shoulders trembled as he continued his story. "When she didn't return to the boarding house I wasn't very upset. I knew she had pawned some shoes of mine and was probably out drinking up the money. I heard on the street that a lady had been arrested for being drunk, and I thought that it might be her."

"Did you check to see if it was Liz?"

"No, because I was too angry. I just went to bed assuming I would find her in the morning. I wish I had gone to the station now."

There wasn't much else Kelly could tell

them and witnesses verified his alibi, so they let him go. Holmes sincerely doubted the true murderer would target someone he was involved with; it would bring him too close to authorities for comfort.

CHAPTER TEN
Broken Letters

Scotland Yard received several other letters over the next few days. Holmes, Inspector Greg, Inspector Smith, and Dr. Watson sat down, going over each one with keen eyes.

The first letter accompanied a mysterious cardboard box. The box contained a half of a human kidney, which later was discovered by the medical records of the coroner to be that of Catherine Eddowes. The letter was dubbed the "from hell" letter and read:

From hell.
Mr. Holmes
Sor
I send you half the kidne I took from one woman and prasarved it for you tother piece I fried and ate it was very nise. I may send you the bloddy knif that took it out if you only wate a whil longer.
Signed
Catch me when you can Mishter Holmes

The appalling spelling set it apart from the other letter they had received—either the sender was not literate or wanted to be perceived that way. *But*, Holmes thought, *why would the writing style change so drastically from the first letter? Is the murderer just toying with us?*

The next letter was intended for the two men, Israel Schwartz and Joseph Lawende, who gave descriptions of the Ripper and were in the immediate vicinity of the killings around the time they happened. This letter was sent to the daily newspaper, which printed it as follows:

You though your-self very clever I reckon when you informed the police. But you made a mistake if you though I dident see you. Now I known you know me and I see your little game, and I mean to finish you and send your ears to your wife if you show this to the police or help them if you do I will finish you. It no use your trying to get out of my way. Because I have you when you don't expect it and I keep my word as you soon see and rip you up.

Yours truly Jack the Ripper

Still, another letter:

Beware I shall be at work on the 1ˢᵗ and 2ⁿᵈ inst. (this means 1ˢᵗ and 2ⁿᵈ of the month of October) *in the Minories at 12 midnight and I*

*give the authorities a good chance but there is never
a policeman near when I am at work.*

Yours Jack the Ripper

Another letter was sent to the coroner
and referred to the kidney sent with the
letter from hell.

*Old box you was rite it was the left kidney I
was goin to hoperate agin close to you ospitle just as
I was going to fror mi nife along of er bloomin throte
them cusses of coppers spoilt the game but I guess I
wil be on the jobn soon and will send you another
but of innerds.*

Jack the Ripper

*O have you seen the delve with his mikerscope
and scalpel a-lookin at a kidney with a slide cocked
up.*

Even a poem was sent. The police were
not sure if it was a hoax.

Eight little whores, with no hope of heaven.

Gladstone may save one, then there'll be seven,

Jack the Ripper

Seven little whores beggin for a shilling.

One stays in Henage Court, then there's a killin.

Six little whores, glad to be alive.

One sidles up to Jack, then there are five.

Four and whore rhyme alright.

So do three and me.

I'll set the town alight

Ere there are two.

Two little whores, shivering with fright.

See a cosy doorway in the middle of the night.

Jack's knife flashes then there's but one.

And the last one's the ripest for Jack's idea of fun.

If the letters and poem were authentic, Holmes had no doubt the Ripper was merely toying with them; it was unlikely they would catch him on the epistles alone. Besides, the handwriting and style of the letters varied so greatly that it was unlikely many of them were authentic. What really preyed on Holmes' mind was why the villain was trying to frame Holmes as the murderer. Holmes was sure that the Ripper was proud of his "work," as he must have seen it, and would want recognition for himself—so why pin it on another?

Holmes was mulling this over as he strolled home in the twilight. When he arrived, he was surprised to see lights blazing in every window; Mrs. Parker was waiting for him on the front stoop, wringing her hands. A few strands of her usually perfectly-coiffed hair had come loose from its bun, and her apron was mussed.

"Mrs. Parker!" Holmes exclaimed. "Whatever is the matter?"

Mrs. Parker jumped to her feet. "Oh, Mr. Holmes!" she cried. "Someone has been in the house—they must have slipped through the back door; you know we always leave it unlocked. I came home early from evening mass, and I noticed the door ajar; I thought it was odd, but went inside."

"Continue, please," said Holmes. "Did you see the intruder? Have you reported this to the police?"

"No, no, I didn't see him," said Mrs. Parker. "And I haven't moved from this front step, I wanted to wait for you!"

Holmes nodded, and she went on with her story. "As soon as I stepped into the kitchen, I heard muffled noises coming from your study. I thought perhaps you had come home early, and I called out for you—but the noises stopped, and then I heard footsteps pounding toward the front door. I froze for a moment in fright, and heard the front door fly open; when I finally worked up the courage to walk down the hall, whoever was here had escaped."

"And then what did you do?" asked Holmes.

"I shut and locked the back door immediately, as well as the front; and then I went through each room of the house to see what the fellow had been after. At first I thought it was a robber, but I thought it odd that the robber would take your best cufflinks and leave your mother's diamond ring; it also appears he took a few handkerchiefs and books from your study. And—sir, this is most upsetting—he left a note on your desk."

At that, Holmes rushed past Mrs. Parker to

his study. His eyes swept the room, noticing its disarray, and he strode to his desk. The note was laid neatly in the center, and the spidery handwriting on it read *"Catch me if you can...JTR."*

Mrs. Parker had followed him inside, and the pallor of her face worried him—she looked as if she might faint. "Has the killer been in our house, sir? How I will get through the days here alone I can't imagine!"

Holmes took Mrs. Parker's elbow and led her back to the kitchen; he started a pot of tea. "You are quite safe," he said. "It does appear the murderer has been here, yes—but you have little if anything in common with his victims. I know you have had a shock, but I would never allow harm to come to you. I will have an officer stroll by the house several times a day, and I will drop by more often as well."

Mrs. Parker nodded, and seemed to calm as she sipped her tea. "Thank you, sir—I appreciate your kindness. What a day!"

Later that night, Holmes held the note and the postcard in front of a candle as if they would reveal their secrets if only he stared at them long enough. He had confirmed Mrs. Parker's suspicions—his cuff links and several of his monogrammed handkerchiefs had been taken, as well as a few slim volumes of poetry. If any of these were left at the scene of the crime…

Finally, he admitted to himself that he should share the information with Inspector Grant—Holmes would never be able to solve the case if he was arrested as the murderer. And he knew, given his own propensity for odd and even erratic behavior, that London society might even believe he had done the crimes.

Nevertheless, something told Holmes to wait—whether it was pride or his natural secretiveness, he did not know. All he did know was that he felt locked in a secret struggle with this murderer, and he refused to admit his fears to another.

CHAPTER ELEVEN
Outside Insides

On November 9, at about 10:45 A.M., John McCarthy, owner of Miller's Court, sent Thomas Bowyer to collect past rent from one of his tenants. He knocked at the door several times and noticed that the door was not locked. He pushed it open, calling the tenant's name, but no response came from within. He stepped into the room and saw a horrific sight: a dead body lying on the bed in a huge pool of blood. Mr. Bowyer turned and ran to tell his boss. The police were notified immediately.

The first policeman to arrive had to be helped out of the room. He became violently ill and was too shaken to stand on his own. The rest of the officers arrived shortly and squeezed into the tiny room; Holmes was among them.

His eyes scanned the room methodically; he saw that the woman's clothing was neatly folded on a chair. Her shoes were paired neatly in front of the fireplace. She had on only her underclothes. That is, what was left of them after all the shredding the knife had done.

The dead woman, Holmes learned from a neighbor, was Mary Jane Kelly, twenty-five years of age. She was about five feet seven inches tall, stout, with blonde hair, blue eyes, and a fair complexion. She was somewhat younger than the other victims and had been killed in a residence rather than on the street, but Holmes still had the feeling this was Jack's work—the state of the body, viciously mutilated, attested to that.

Holmes had already explored the room the best he could to see if there was anything of a personal nature in the room. He was also quite pleased at all the untouched surfaces in the room, and took his time dusting the table, chairs, and other objects for fingerprints.

At the end of his explorations he found, lying partway under the victim's body, the thumb section of a glove. A doctor's glove? He turned it over to a detective, thinking to himself that this was one more clue that the murderer was in the medical profession.

Holmes decided to use this time to visit the neighbors and see if he could find out anything about the poor woman's last hours. This should make the investigation go a little faster, since most of the witnesses were in one rooming house.

Holmes stopped a uniformed policeman. "You can be of immense help to this investigation," he said, handing the man his notebook. "Please come along with me and take notes as I interview possible witnesses— that way, I can focus on my questions and the answers. Write down your own impressions, too—there could be one hundred men watching an interview and each would observe something different."

Within a few hours, Holmes found out that Mary Jane was a nice, quiet woman who was well-liked by others. Though she could become boisterous when drinking, for the most part she never caused any trouble and got along well with everyone.

Lizzie Albrook, a neighbor, told of her last interactions with Mary Jane. "We were together last night at the bar. We had quite a long talk about life. She told me not to end up as she had. She was sad that her life was what it was, and she wished she could go to Ireland to live with family. She had to resort to her kind of life so she wouldn't starve," Lizzie said. "We parted when a man appeared at her side. I couldn't tell you anything about him though, because I had someone myself."

"Thank you, Miss Albrook. If you think of anything else, please let us know," Holmes said as he passed her his card.

Mary Ann Cox was another neighbor who readily answered the questions put to her. She offered Holmes and his assistant a cup of tea, which they refused.

"When did you last see the victim?" Holmes asked.

"It was last night. I was walking home and she was walking in front of me with a man. They went into her room and I wished them goodnight."

"How did she act?"

"She looked intoxicated, to be honest, but she did bid me goodnight. I thought it was strange she started singing in her room, but alcohol makes us all do funny things. I went out about 1:00 A.M. and she was still singing. I came back about 3:00 A.M. and the singing had stopped, and the lights of her room were out."

"Can you describe the man she was with?" Holmes asked.

"He looked to be about thirty-six years old and stood about five feet five inches tall. He had a red moustache and small side-whiskers. His face looked a little red to me. He had on dark clothing with a dark overcoat and a black hat."

"Did he appear drunk? And had you seen him before?"

"I could not tell if he was drunk, sir. But I did not sleep that night with all of the murder talk going around, and I thought I heard him leave around 6 A.M. As for recognizing him, Mary Jane had frequent visitors—I didn't pay much attention to anyone's faces."

Mary Ann's niece happened to be home that night as well. "I saw Mary Jane and her caller from my door," the niece said. "He was a nice-looking fellow—like he was rich, you know—and he had on a cape and a top hat. He was carrying a bag, too—a Gladstone bag."

"Do you remember anything else?"

The niece shuddered. "Aunt Mary Ann said she heard someone scream 'murder!' late in the night—I didn't hear it myself, and I'm glad of it!"

"I heard no such thing," interrupted Mary Ann. "My niece is an excitable young woman—this situation has unsettled her nerves, I dare say."

Holmes thanked them for their somewhat contradicting reports and returned to the room where the murder had occurred. He was glad to see that the coroner's office had carried the body away and he was doubly happy to see the face of his old friend walking toward him.

"Watson, I am so glad you are here. This young man has been so kind as to help me jot down my interviews, but I am sure you will take over his job now," Holmes said.

"Of course, I will be pleased to do it," Dr. Watson answered as he took the notebook from the young officer, who seemed happy to depart.

"Have you found anything promising in today's work?"

"Not much. I'm just deciphering the conflicting information from the witnesses. Do people ever really open their eyes?" Holmes laughed. "I suppose if they did, then Scotland Yard and detectives like myself wouldn't be necessary."

"One would assume people would be more observant at a time like this, at least," Dr. Watson replied. "Their lives may depend on it."

The men walked down the hall to the next room, where they encountered a woman.

"Excuse me, but did you know the victim?"

Dr. Watson asked.

"Yes sir."

"How?"

"Well, I do laundry here for the tenants and happened to spend the night last night. I went to Mary Jane's room to pick up some clothes. We were friends, so we had a little drink together," the woman told them. "The last time I saw Mary Jane alive was when she left about half past seven on her way to the corner bar."

"Was she intoxicated when you parted ways?"

"No," the woman answered simply. "I must say, I'm so shocked to hear about this— Mary Jane was a good, kind girl. I can't imagine anyone wanting to hurt her!"

Julia Venturney was another neighbor who had known Mary about four months.

"Tell us anything you know about her," Holmes urged. "Not just about the last time you saw her, but about how she lived."

Well," started Julia, "She lived with Joe Barnett—at least for a while. He was angry, quite angry, at how Mary earned her living— when she started taking to the streets regularly, Joe moved out. He said he'd come back when she stopped living that kind of life."

"Were they still together?" asked Holmes. "As a couple, I mean."

"As far as I know," answered Julia. "He came to visit her almost every night, and he brought her money when he could—but he just refused to live with her. She told me more than once how it hurt her, but she didn't know any other way to get by."

"Did you hear any strange noises last night?" Holmes asked.

"Nothing out of the ordinary—no screams or struggles, if that's what you mean."

"I am ready to take a break," Holmes told Dr. Watson as they walked away from Julia. "I have been at this for a long time and need a hearty meal to see me through the rest of the day."

The men walked down the stairs and out into the bright sunshine. There were still many people standing around watching the house. As they neared the sidewalk Holmes saw a short, stocky man who looked familiar to him.

CHAPTER TWELVE
Plan in Review

"Mr. Hamilton," Holmes said to the man in the suit, inclining his head slightly to acknowledge the presence of his friend.

"Hello Detective," Donald Hamilton said to him.

"I am not used to seeing you dressed in everyday attire. What brought you here today?"

"Well, I was not working today and I heard of the new murder. I wanted to see where it took place. I guess I am playing amateur detective in trying to solve these cases. I see the dead, but rarely the site of the killings," Hamilton told them.

"Have you noticed anything suspicious?" Holmes asked.

"No, not really. I have seen several men standing around, but most of them are probably old clients, friends, or merely spectators drawn by the tragedy."

"Well, if you see anything out of the ordinary, please let me know. You know where I am most hours of the day," Holmes said. "Both Dr. Watson and I have burned more than our share of midnight oil in the past few weeks."

"He could be a big help to you," Dr. Watson told his friend as they left the boarding house. "Do you trust him?"

"As much as I trust anyone right now, my friend—which is to say, 'no.' But that does not mean he cannot be my ears inside the coroner's office."

"You are a master of getting information out of people without them fully realizing they are giving it," said Dr. Watson. "It's a skill I have always admired."

The men took Dr. Watson's carriage to their favorite pub in the heart of London. They ordered a good lunch and talked about the case. There was a staggering amount of information to review and more witnesses to interrogate. Holmes still needed to review the list of suspects, and the witness' contradicting statements about the possible perpetrator's appearance were frustrating. Most of the witnesses had said he was short with a mustache, but some said he was well-dressed, and others said he was not. Some reported he had been carrying a bag or other object, and some said he had not been carrying anything. Even worse, Holmes knew that the descriptions could be completely useless—the man (or men) described might have been clients, rather than the killer.

Holmes decided for the time being to focus on the coroner's report on the latest victim. Mary Jane was the first to have been killed inside a dwelling. That made it unique. She was lying on the bed, her head turned to the left, as were all the others. Her left arm was across her stomach, with the right arm outstretched to the right across the mattress. Her legs were spread apart with knees bent. The entirety of her insides had been scooped out, her breasts had been cut off, and she had many jagged incisions on her body from a knife. Her organs were laying around her body…her liver between her feet, a breast under her arm…it was all arranged to create a horrific scene. The killer had really done a job on this poor woman.

Her face had been mutilated, made unrecognizable. Her neck, hands, and legs were covered in gashes. Almost every inch of her body was grotesquely mutilated as if she were a piece of meat. She had almost been skinned. It must have taken hours. Her last meal had been fish and potatoes and was partially digested. The carotid artery had been sliced while she lay on her side, and it was this cut that had caused her death, also leaving a large puddle of blood.

"I have an idea, Watson."

"What might that be?"

"I would like to see if a friend of one of the victims might help us set up the murderer. I don't want anyone from the police to know about it, because we do not know if any of them are involved in the murders," Holmes said. "I hate to say that, but it is the truth. The murderer could be anybody."

"I dare say."

"I want to get a woman to walk the streets near where the victims were found and see if we can attract him. Of course, I will be counting on you to help me keep her safe."

"Of course. So we will be using someone as a lure?"

"Yes, though I shudder to call a human being that."

"Who will it be?"

"I have in mind a woman named Julie, a good friend of Mary Ann Nichols. She has been in touch with me several times and wants to help. I'm sure she will be willing to do what is asked of her."

"How soon will we set this plan into action?"

"Well, I will require a few more days to go over the information we have so far. I will call upon Julie to propose this idea—do you have the afternoon free to come along?"

"I am always at your service," said Dr. Watson.

The two men paid their bill and returned to the dark, winding streets of Whitechapel to find Julie. She lived in a shabby lodging house, and Holmes and Dr. Watson waited patiently in the parlor for the landlady to fetch her. They both rose to greet her.

"I hope we have not inconvenienced you by arriving unannounced," said Holmes. "But you see, I've had an idea—and I immediately thought of you as the one person who can help us."

"If your idea will result in the capture of the Ripper, I am completely at your disposal," answered Julie. "I've cried every night over Polly—I barely sleep thinking of what happened to her. I want her murder avenged, and I don't want any other innocent women to face that knife."

Holmes smiled in relief. "I was hoping you would say that, my dear. Here's what we had in mind…"

CHAPTER THIRTEEN
Gripped in Fear

Several men came into Scotland Yard claiming to be Jack the Ripper—most were drunk when they confessed to the crimes, and the police immediately dismissed them. Rumors flew around the city, growing more outlandish every day. Everyone suspected everyone—family turned against family, friend against friend, neighbor against neighbor. As the panic gripping London increased, Holmes found himself with a growing number of stories and alibis to go through—no matter how unlikely, every accusation had to be studied.

Yet Holmes suffered through many of the confessions and reports with irritated disbelief—he was quite aware that such a situation brought out the strangest members of society, but still—they were idling away time that could be better spent on any number of tasks.

Joseph Barnett, Mary Jane's occasional live-in lover, immediately became a suspect. Though he was not residing with Mary at the time, Holmes knew from Julia that their relationship had continued—and it was a union filled with conflict. Joseph was not only livid that Mary Jane sold her body to make a living, but they also fought constantly about Mary Jane's soft heart when it came to her friends; she would let almost anyone stay with her when they had no place else to go for the night.

"But if Barnett was angry with Mary, so angry that he would commit murder, why would he not just kill Mary?" asked Dr. Watson. "Why would he kill the other women first? I must say I don't see any motivation there."

"He may have committed those murders to scare Mary off the streets," Holmes answered. "Thwarted passion can drive a man to commit heinous acts—especially if he is already unbalanced. And his vivisection of the bodies certainly aligns with the rage he feels toward the occupation of prostitution in general. But—"

Dr. Watson finished the sentence. "He has no medical training that we know of; and the murderer must have some knowledge of human anatomy."

There were other suspects, of course, based on the profile Holmes had drafted—but additional problems arose based on the contradicting descriptions of the murderer. The accounts of his appearance varied substantially, and as Holmes told himself again and again, many of the men described could merely have been soliciting services with nothing so vile as murder in mind.

The only thing to do, Holmes had definitively decided, was to lure the murderer out with a vulnerable woman— and catch him before she became the next victim. They would need help, though, if they were to catch Jack—they must convince Grant to go along with their plan. Other than Holmes, he was the sharpest detective in the city.

Holmes called a meeting that afternoon. "We have something to discuss with you," Holmes told Grant. "We have devised a plan and need your help."

"Well certainly. You know you have free rein concerning the Ripper case—anything you need that I can provide will be at your fingertips. I know that sometimes you are rather—ahem—unorthodox in solving cases, and I assure you I am open to anything to catch the beast stalking our city."

Holmes explained the gist of the plan and sat back to

await Grant's response.

"But where will we find a woman willing to help us carry out this plan—one who is willing to risk her own life?"

"We have already found such a woman," Holmes said solemnly. "And she understands the ramifications of what she has agreed to do. We can schedule a meeting to continue our planning at my residence on Baker Street. If the murderer is an officer or detective who walks among us now, we do not want him learning of our plot and ruining it."

"We can keep this outside of Scotland Yard," agreed Grant. "However, I will ask that I bring in two policemen who I trust to help us. We cannot carry out your idea without proper protection, both for ourselves and for the young woman. I promise they will satisfy your expectations of discretion."

"As long as you are assured the men are trustworthy, I will not doubt your word," said Holmes. "Though I would ensure they have alibis for the nights of the murders before you tell them any details about our plan—just to be safe."

"Then let's plan to meet at your house tomorrow night at six. Please get in touch with the woman and let her know that Scotland Yard—and all of London—appreciates the sacrifice she is making."

"I shall, sir."

CHAPTER FOURTEEN

Society of Secrets

For the remainder of the day, Holmes and Watson studied the coroner's reports and information gathered by the officers. Dr. Watson made notes when Holmes indicated that he do so. They needed to understand every detail of how the murders had occurred before they put their plan to work.

It seemed likely that, in most if not all of the cases, the murderer had made sure the victims' hands were occupied before he committed his crime. The women had lifted their skirts for sex, busying their hands, and then the culprit had strangled them while they could not defend themselves. Some had died from the strangulation, while others just passed out before he brought out the knife. That was why there was no screaming for passersby to hear. The murderer was very cunning. He had to convince the victim he wanted to procure her services—perhaps he even proffered coins, which he would take back after the woman was dead.

He would then lower them to the ground, their heads to his left. He had not dropped them roughly, for there was no bruising. In this way, he could reach over and cut their throats from left to right with the blood draining to the left away from him. In one case, some blood had been found on the nearby fence, sprayed from the woman's artery, but nothing appeared to have interrupted its flow—so it had not gotten on the murderer. The fellow had some sort of medical knowledge, of that Holmes remained sure. *Is this monster someone I know?* he wondered. *Is it a medical student, or a doctor, or even a butcher?*

"He is a very smart man," Holmes told Dr. Watson.

"He is carrying out these murders flawlessly—if there is a drop of blood on him or a hair out of place when he's done, I would be surprised."

"Yes, I see he is very cunning—and devilishly hard to catch," Dr. Watson answered. "The thing is, why is he trying to bring you under suspicion? I am sure that is never far from your mind. Does he want to blame you? Does he want you to catch him because he knows you are the best detective in our great country, if not the world?"

"It struck me this morning, as I shaved," answered Holmes. "Many of my insights come to me during that mundane task. Think to yourself of the most important connection I have—of an esteemed friend who shaped my investigative skill."

Watson gasped. "Edmond Dantes! You're not saying—"

Holmes laughed. "Of course I am not saying it is Dantes! But this crime must have something to do with the Sovereign Order of Monte Cristo—there are several secret societies that splintered off from the Illuminati, and those societies wish Dantes and all of his friends and companions ill. It is common knowledge now that Dantes got me started on this path, which led me to become the brilliant detective I am today—so who better to target than myself? I am sure a member of another society is behind this. "

"I think you've come to a scarily accurate conclusion about the murderer," agreed Dr. Watson. "But the person could be anyone—anywhere. Do you have any suspects now that you've uncovered this link?"

"Yes, I am compiling a list that you and I will go over. I am eliminating each suspect by a laborious process of deductive reasoning—it is time-consuming, but fruitful. However, my musings will be for your ears only, my friend."

"You need not say another word about that," Dr. Watson assured him.

"I must tell you, though, that I got another note this morning. It was laying on my desk, right here at Scotland Yard."

"What did it say?"

Holmes pulled the note from his pocket and read it aloud. *"You can't hide…but I can. Have I baffled even your great mind? JTR."*

"I am beginning to think this fellow has an accomplice," Dr. Watson said. "How could he so easily slip into this building, unnoticed, unless he is one of the officers?"

"That is why the less men who are involved, the better. The murderer could very well be a detective or an officer who is exceptionally wily—someone we would never expect. This would be a game to them if so."

"A game with grisly trophies," shuddered Dr. Watson. "And where does the monster keep these body parts he takes? There has only been one victim from whom he didn't take entrails; yet he touched none of them in a sexual manner. And he commits his dastardly acts in the dead of night, so swiftly that he is probably nearby when the body is found—yet he is not yet caught. I don't understand it."

"Watson, has anyone in Scotland Yard made you feel in any way suspicious? Or even at the morgue? I must say, since I began receiving these notes I often feel as if we are being watched," Holmes said.

"I can't say that I have. But, then again, we are always surrounded by others here, and we are often too absorbed in work to notice anyone acting out of sorts."

"I just get the distinct feeling lately that someone is always on my trail. The killer could be right beside us, and we might never know. He is not leaving any clues to his identity—though he has no compunction about leaving clues to mine."

"I know, my friend. This is a hard one," Dr. Watson said as he patted Holmes on the shoulder.

"We should put our plan into motion immediately. Tomorrow night we will have our meeting with Grant, our decoy, and the men Grant chooses to join us. I do hope he has the utmost faith in the pair he picks. I don't want to take any chances that the murderer hears of our plan and evades capture. We have to stop this monster before someone else gets killed."

When Holmes arrived at the house on Baker Street that night, Mrs. Parker was in good spirits, humming and smiling. However, when Holmes retreated to his office and saw what was on his desk, he felt he would not smile for a long time. There, sitting on a household ledger, was one of his missing handkerchiefs.

It was covered in blood, now dried and brown, but he could still make out his initials stitched in blue thread...SH.

The killer could have left it at the scene, Holmes thought, *but he wants me to know he has the power here, the upper hand—both on the streets and even in my own home. This is unacceptable.*

He swept the handkerchief into a drawer; he would burn it as soon as possible. And then he would resume his investigation with a vengeance.

CHAPTER FIFTEEN
True Suspects

Though deeply unsettled, Holmes forced himself to concentrate only on the case. When he finished his list of suspects to his satisfaction, he began the process of validating or eliminating each one. He posted the list on the wall for all to see, and called the detectives around him. He then read out the list as follows:

JACK THE RIPPER SUSPECTS

- Prince Albert Victor
- Joseph Barnett
- Alfred Blanchard
- William Henry Bury
- Lewis Carroll
- David Cohen
- Dr. Thomas Neill Cream
- Frederick Bailey Deeming
- Montague John Druitt
- Carl Ferdinand Feigenbaum
- George Hutchinson
- Hyam Hyams
- Jill the Ripper
- James Kelly
- George Chapman
- Aaron Kosminski
- Jacob Levy

- James Maybrick
- Michael Ostrog
- Dr. Alexander Pedachenko
- Walter Sickert
- James Kenneth Stephen
- Robert D'Onston Stephenson
- Francis Thompson
- Francis Tumblety
- Alois Szemeredy
- Nikolay Vasiliev
- Dr. John Williams

"I have gathered you all here together to see this list of suspects," he said. "Each detective will be responsible for investigating certain names on the list—and all information obtained must be reported immediately to me. I will be working diligently as well, and together we will apprehend Jack the Ripper.

"You may feel overwhelmed by the number of names on the list—but your hard work and keen observation could lead to the discovery of the murderer's identity. Remember to work with the theoretical profile developed through my expertise. Check the dates and times of alibis. Be thorough in what you do. And do not be sure that it is only one man committing the murders. There may be a partner. Another murder may occur at any time, so we must make haste," Holmes concluded.

One of the officers called out, "What about the rumors that Jack is a Jill? I notice there are no women on the list."

"Of course, we must investigate every possibility," said

Holmes. "But it is unlikely any woman would have the strength or stamina to commit such brutally violent murders. Jill the Ripper is not a viable possibility—at least at this time."

Even though Holmes had some peculiar ways, and often spoke curtly and coldly, nearly everyone at Scotland Yard liked and respected him. He had solved countless cases in his lifetime, and they all wanted to learn from the man they considered the master. In most cases, though, they knew Holmes kept his suspect near and dear to him until he could prove without a doubt who it was. They all wondered if he already had his suspicions—and if they could beat him to the discovery of the Ripper's true identity.

The detectives lined up and Holmes gave each man a list of three or four suspects. He had a special list of his own, which he would begin investigating immediately. His list included not only facts about each suspect, but also his own notes and opinions.

- James Kelly

James Kelly was raised by his grandmother, who he thought to be his mother. His birth mother, who had no interest in raising her own child, married Kelly's father even though he did not know she had given birth to his son. Later in life, after Kelly's father died, his mother left Kelly the money that her husband had willed her. She felt remorse for what she had done. She died shortly after that.

As an adult, Kelly worked as an upholsterer and lived in lodging houses. He met his wife, Sarah, in 1881. He lived in the same lodging house as Sarah, who shared the space with her parents and siblings. He grew angry early in the courtship because he and Sarah had little opportunity for privacy, so he began frequenting prostitutes and contracted a venereal disease. His behavior became erratic, but in 1883 Sarah and Kelly still wed. Gossip said that they never consummated their union, due to the fact that Sarah was a virgin and Kelly could not penetrate her. He believed she had a deformity, and their relationship continued to deteriorate.

His disease soon led to horrible headaches and discharge from his ears, and eventually his mother-in-law found the drugs and syringes he used to treat his syphilis. Kelly became enraged and tried to blame Sarah for his affliction, and even accused her of tricking him into marriage to get his inheritance for herself.

Despite his anger toward her, Kelly was consumed with jealousy over Sarah, and once threatened her with a knife. On another occasion, his rage overcame him, and he stabbed Sarah and dragged her by the hair out of the house. She died from her injuries, and he was arrested for murder. He was sentenced to be hanged, but his sentence was overturned. He was declared to be insane and sentenced to an asylum, but escaped and fled to London.

<u>Reasons for considering James Kelly as a suspect</u>: Kelly was diagnosed as a Paranoid Schizophrenic and killed his wife with a knife, confirming his capacity for brutal violence. He believed his wife was a prostitute or at least unchaste, and connected his own illness with her in his mind. The current murders could be Kelly's twisted way of taking revenge for his own plight. Also damning—he lived with Catherine Eddowes for a time.

Unfortunately, Kelly does not match descriptions of the Ripper, if indeed those descriptions are accurate. The Ripper has been described as five foot seven inches tall, with a dark complexion, black hair, a heavy mustache, and a thin, pale face. Despite that, I still consider him a suspect.

- George Chapman

George Chapman was born Antoniovich Klosowski in Poland, and pursued a career as a surgeon in his home country before immigrating to America, at which time he found employment as a hairdresser's assistant.

He married a woman named Lucy Baderski despite already being married, and his first wife left Poland and the three lived together for a time in London. Eventually, Chapman's first wife left, but Chapman's marriage to Lucy was fraught with unhappiness. They often fought, and at one point Chapman attacked Lucy with a knife. He was also known to beat other women with whom he had a relationship.

<u>Reasons for considering James Chapman as a suspect</u>: Chapman has a steady and regular job, and so would likely only have been free on the weekends to commit murders—which is when Jack the Ripper strikes. He also lives in the immediate area of the murders. Now that his wives have left him, he is single and has no responsibility, so he can come and go as he pleases with no questions. His wife noted he often stayed out until the early morning hours, and revealed he once threatened to cut off her head.

Chapman is also said to have a voracious sexual appetite, but at the same time is very hostile toward women. Perhaps this hostility, combined with his lust, could drive him to murder.

Despite these possibilities, however, Chapman is around twenty-three years old, and the descriptions we've received of Jack the Ripper put him at thirty-five to forty years of age. Additionally, the Ripper is reported to act and sound like an educated man, while Chapman is an immigrant. It also seems peculiar that, given Chapman's sexual drive, he did not actually have intercourse with any of the victims if indeed he is the Ripper.

- William Henry Bury

Not much has been uncovered about Bury, though he did murder his late wife, Ellen—by strangulation, with stab wounds to the abdomen after her death. Bury sleeps with a penknife under his pillow, and "Jack the Ripper is in this cellar" was written in chalk upon his door.

<u>Reasons to consider William Henry Bury as a suspect</u>: Ellen's stab wounds were very similar to those of the first victim, Polly Nichols; furthermore, Ellen was a former prostitute.

While there are connections, I do not believe Bury is a true candidate for Jack the Ripper.

- Jacob Levy

Jacob Levy is a Jewish butcher who lives with his wife near the scene of the murders. He has a history of mental illness in his family, and is believed to be unstable himself. Levy has been uncooperative with the investigation.

<u>Reasons to consider William Henry Bury as a suspect</u>: A fellow butcher reported seeing Bury with Catharine Eddowes on the night

of her murder; Bury would have had enough knowledge of anatomy from his trade to cleanly and efficiently mutilate his victims. Additionally, a witness claims to have seen a man of Jewish appearance with Mary Jane Kelly in the vicinity of her murder.

- Dr. John Williams

Sir John Williams was raised by his mother, who ran the family farm on her own after her husband's death. He initially studied religion, but later apprenticed himself to a surgeon and went on to study medicine. He attended the University College Hospital in London to procure his medical and surgeon's degree. He married Elisabeth Ann Hughes in 1872, and they subsequently had issues conceiving. He studied as an obstetric physician as a result of their fertility problems, and eventually established an impressive reputation in the field.

<u>Reasons to consider Dr. John Williams as a suspect</u>: According to a relative, Dr. John Williams allegedly knows one of the victims, Mary Kelly, and it has been suggested he was "seeing" her. The same relative attested to seeing a three-sided knife that he swore was the Ripper's weapon, and claimed that Dr. Williams was very invested in performing experiments that could unlock the secret of why he and his wife could not have a child. Dr. Williams also performed an abortion on Mary Ann Nichols, another victim.

While one could surmise that Dr. Williams carried out the murders to harvest body parts for his experiments, as a respected doctor he could just have easily carried out these experiments on unclaimed cadavers in the morgue. He also has no history of violence or instability; his connection to the victims seems mere circumstance. Further, the murderer seems to be taunting me, and to take a sick glee in his "work"—it seems unlikely that a man murdering to carry out experiments would act in so unclinical a fashion. I do not seriously consider him a suspect.

- Aaron Kosminski

Aaron Kosminksi is a Polish Jew who only recently emigrated to England; he works as a hairdresser in Whitechapel.

Reasons to consider Aaron Kosminski as a suspect: Kosminksi is known to be mentally ill, and several witnesses have said he displays a hatred toward women. As a Jew, he could very likely be in league with a group that opposes the Sovereign Order of Monte Cristo, which is a Christian society.

CHAPTER SIXTEEN
The Set Up

Holmes eagerly prepared his house for the meeting. He knew it would be a long and tedious one, but he was sure they would all be quite comfortable in his study. Mrs. Parker had outdone herself to ensure they would not go hungry—delicious scents wafted from the kitchen, and she was prepared to serve the meal as soon as their visitors arrived.

She had baked a ham with pineapples and brown sugar dripping off the platter, and roasted a chicken, with mushroom stuffing on the side. Corn on the cob, drenched with butter, sat alongside blanched green beans, baked potatoes, and fresh-baked bread. She had coffee brewed, tea steeping, and ale on hand as well. Holmes remembered why he had hired her.

"I extend my thanks to you, Mrs. Parker. You are an amazing woman."

"You're welcome, sir. I know this is a very important meeting, and I know you all will more than likely be here until well into the night," she answered. "I have two apple pies in the oven and a chocolate cake already baked. I have even arranged to spend the night here, so I can serve you all as needed."

"You must remind me to give you a raise, Mrs. Parker," said Holmes.

"Oh, I will…I will," she answered with a sly smile.

Dr. Watson arrived right on time, and he and Holmes were enjoying their pipes when the others arrived.

Julie was a very attractive woman. She was in her late

twenties and had long, auburn hair, half of which was swept up into a bun while the other half tumbled down her back. Holmes hoped she would make the perfect decoy—though the Ripper's first victims had been older, the murder of Mary Jane Kelly had shown he would be willing to attack younger women as well.

"Welcome to my home," he said, bowing over her hand. "Inspector Grant, allow me to formally introduce Miss Julie Rivers."

Inspector Grant, though not used to treating a woman of the night as a lady, was nonetheless gracious. He inclined his head to her and smiled. "It is a pleasure to meet such a brave woman as yourself."

"Thank you. I appreciate that you have included me in this meeting. I want to do everything that I can to help catch Mary Ann's killer."

Inspector Grant then introduced the two policemen he had brought with him.

"May I present Thomas Hunter and Joseph Jackson," he said as he waved his hand from one to the other. "I have known these men for over thirty years and would trust them with my life. We grew up together."

"Thank you, Thomas and Joseph, for your assistance—and discretion," Holmes told them.

"You are quite welcome. We are most happy to assist you in solving this case, sir," said Thomas, the shorter of the two.

"Yes, anything we can do to help," Joseph responded.

"I believe this to be the most singular case of my career," Holmes replied. "And with every day that passes, the stakes grow higher—we must catch this murderer before he slays another victim. First, though, we eat—I've found that full stomachs lead to sharper, less distracted minds."

The smell of the food was indeed inviting, and the group retreated to the garden to dine. It was a fine meal, and their conversation remained focused on trivial matters.

When the last plate was cleared, however, Holmes rose to his feet. "And now it is time to get down to business," he said. "Please follow me to my study—I have made some notes for each of you in regard to the profile I've created, and I've included several key points on the case. We will discuss the suspects, as well as lay out our plan for catching the Ripper."

In the study, everyone took a seat and solemnly accepted the sheaves of paper Holmes handed them. "The only way for us to catch this villain is to set a trap. Mind you, it could be dangerous—even deadly—so if you are having second thoughts about participating, you must speak now."

Nobody said a word.

"Good," Holmes nodded. "It may seem indecorous to discuss the Ripper's crimes in the presence of a woman, but Julie knows her role and is willing to act as a lure, despite the danger."

"We will never be far from you, Julie, so please try not to worry too much," Grant said.

"Oh, I am not worried. I trust you will keep me safe. I just hope the killer will take the bait…me," she said with a nervous laugh.

"We will start with Julie in the Top Star Bar, the pub most of the women visited before their murders. Of course we will need either Joseph and Thomas there too, keeping an eye on her," Holmes started. "It seems the pub may be the starting point where the killer first sees his victim. The victims left a little, or even a lot, intoxicated. I will speak with the bar keeper, Julie, and tell him to give you seltzer water instead of liquor."

"I may want just one for courage and something on my breath," Julie said. "I will feign clumsiness and spill some of on my dress, as well."

"That will be your final drink," said Grant. "Holmes and myself will hide behind the white fence that lines the sidewalk from the bar to Whitechapel, and we will station one of the officers in the bar to watch you. Dr. Watson will be up the street somewhere, keeping an eye from afar."

"Yes, and we will be dressed as if we belong in the neighborhood, so as not to raise suspicion. Remember, Julie, we will not be far from you at any time. You need to give us some sort signal, though, if you suspect that you have the fish on the line," Holmes told her. "You have the profile, so you must redirect the attention of anyone who does not fit it. Can you do that?"

"Yes sir. I will be able to do that. And if I feel I have him I will say, where you all can hear, 'I am getting a little chilled—I wish I had brought my wrap!'"

"Excellent! But of course you know he will have to make some kind of move to hurt you—and for that to happen, you will have to lead him outside. That's what will make it so dangerous."

"I understand. I will leave the pub with the man only if I am sure he is the Ripper."

They all went through several possible scenarios so that everyone would be prepared for anything that might happen. For hours they did this, until they could no longer keep their eyes open. They agreed they would go out the next evening about 10 P.M. They knew that apprehending the murderer might take more than one night, but they were prepared to be patient.

Holmes and Watson spoke at the door as Watson was leaving.

"You suspect who it is don't you, my friend?" Dr. Watson said. "Your demeanor has grown calm and composed—as if a weight has been lifted from your shoulders. I feel as if you've had another of your famous epiphanies sometime this night."

"Yes, I am almost sure, I do but I do not want to disclose his identity right now, even to you."

"I understand these feelings you get. We will catch him, Holmes."

CHAPTER SEVENTEEN
The Hours Before

The next day was a long and tiring one. Each member of group not only had to prepare for his or her part of the plan, but also toil at their day job. Julie engaged a few of her friends to help her dress, and though she was nervous about the coming danger being around others lightened her mood and made the time pass quickly.

Holmes worked on his list alone, as he had requested that Dr. Watson stay home and rest—when Holmes neared his quarry, he preferred the peace of solitude. Holmes was not the only detective who had made progress, however—quite a few suspects had been eliminated by the others working on the case. The list was slowly shortening, and while Holmes was almost certain he now knew the perpetrator, he wanted to leave no doubt in his own mind. As a result, he continued to investigate every remaining suspect.

Just as Holmes was diving deep into concentration, his train of thought was broken by the friendly voice of Donald, from the coroner's office.

"I trust you are having a pleasant day, Inspector Holmes?"

"It is busy, but certainly it has not been a bad day. I feel we are getting ever closer to catching the Ripper."

"The whole city hopes so. We are grateful that there have been no other murders yet. The dedicated work of Scotland Yard must have the fellow on the run, sir."

"I certainly hope so. We need a break in the case,

though, to pin the monster down. Have you discovered anything else that might be of use to us in your examinations?"

"No, not yet. You do know of the piece of glove that was found?"

"Yes, I found it myself."

"Then nothing else as of yet. If there is anything at all I can do to assist with this case, please do not hesitate to ask me. I am at your service."

"I appreciate your offer, but I believe we have the situation under control. Inspector Grant and I have circulated a suspect list to the other detectives, and we are all hard at work eliminating those who are innocent."

"A list!" Donald exclaimed. "How fascinating—would you mind terribly if I had a look?"

Holmes smiled. "It is, of course, confidential. I am sure you understand the delicacy of this investigation."

"Of course. I understand. Well, I had better return to work."

"Thank you for coming by, Donald. I'm sure we will meet again soon."

Then Inspector Grant walked over and interrupted Holmes as well. *It seems to be a theme of the afternoon*, Holmes thought irritably.

"Are you ready for tonight?" Grant asked in a low voice.

"I hope so. We will each decide where we will be standing when Julie takes her walk. That will be the most important thing. That white picket fence will be perfect. It is by the bar, but still cast in shadow. I will have Watson waiting up the street a ways—inconspicuously, of course."

"Yes, and I will station one officer in the bar and

another in the alley. I must remind everyone to dress as if they are local workers and maybe carry a bottle of whiskey with them so they will blend in," Grant grinned. "Then you and I can take up the picket fence."

"Yes."

"I must commend you on the suspect list. The men are working diligently on it. I think we have made some real progress," Grant said. "I, myself, cannot wait to see who this filthy culprit is. Do you have a clue yet?"

"I do, but I always prefer to keep silent until I am absolutely sure."

"I respect that. Let's just get him caught."

"Of course, my friend. I will see you tonight at the bar."

With that, they parted company and Holmes prepared to return to Baker Street. He wanted to enjoy a light supper and a short nap.

CHAPTER EIGHTEEN
Swing and Miss

Thomas Hunter settled himself at a table in the bar, pretending to nurse a glass of whiskey, and Joseph Jackson lurked in the first alley after the white picket fence. They had each dressed down to look like laborers and each played his part excellently. They were all eyes and ears.

Julie also looked perfect for the night's task. She wore a crimson dress, which dipped low in the front to show her collarbone and the creamy flesh of her cleavage. Her hair was swept up, a red rose securing it behind one ear, and her face was heavily made up to accentuate her full lips and large, lovely eyes.

Inspector Grant settled himself behind the white picket fence behind the pub, and as he saw Dr. Watson go by he hissed, "Sir! Yes, you sir."

Dr. Watson looked around himself to make sure no one was observing them, but the only fellow he saw was a vagrant, passed out against the fence.

"I thought I was to wait further down the road?"

"Yes, yes—but where is Holmes? He is supposed to be here with us."

Dr. Watson looked concerned. "I do not know—it is not like him to be late. Should I send a messenger to his house? I could perhaps pay someone in the pub to take a missive."

"No, that would draw attention to us," Inspector Grant said. "I suppose we will just carry on with our plan and hope he appears."

Just then, the drunk sleeping on the street gave a snort that sounded strangely like a chuckle. The fellow lurched to his feet and pulled a shining pipe from his pocket; he placed a small amount of tobacco in the bowl and tamped it.

"Could I bother you blokes for a match?" the man said—and it was then that Dr. Watson realized the tramp was his old friend and partner, Sherlock Holmes!

"Why, it's you!" Dr. Watson gasped, laughing in shock. "You are wholly unrecognizable!"

Indeed, Holmes' own mother would not have recognized the man; though he was usually impeccably groomed and garbed, now he was dressed in a tattered overcoat and his face and hands were smeared with grime.

Holmes did not break character for a second. "If you've no match on you, then I'll sit myself down again," he said, slipping the pipe into his pocket and resuming his post.

Dr. Watson continued his walk to a nearby alley, and Inspector Grant gazed with admiration upon Holmes—he knew he was in the presence of greatness whenever that man was near.

Inside the pub, Thomas had instructed the bartender to give Julie only seltzer water after the first drink; assuming Thomas was her pimp and perhaps used to such requests, he readily complied. Julie slowly began to act as if the liquor had gone to her head, and soon men began to gravitate toward her. She rebuffed them one by one based on their appearance, and made sure to mingle with the other women in the bar as well. At 1 A.M., when no one who resembled the suspect had approached her, she stumbled out into the night alone (though watched closely by those around her).

Holmes and Grant were alert and ready when Julie left the bar. They each went to opposite sides of the fence so they could watch her better. She was to stop along the way, talk to men, and see if the Ripper tried to target her. So far, nobody of Jack's description had made a pass at her.

She stopped, leaning against the edge of an alcove to a store, pretending to dig through the small satchel at her waist. A man of average build strolled over and attempted to engage her in conversation. Holmes and Grant could not quite hear what he was saying, but the look on Julie's face told them she did not feel she was in danger. More men, none matching the description, approached her as the night dragged on. And it was a long one. The Ripper either knew something was up or he was taking the night off. At about 6:00 A.M. the group went home, still in character so nobody would notice.

They gathered around lunchtime the next day at Baker Street, discussing the night before.

"None of the men matched the description of the Ripper," Grant said solemnly. "It might take weeks to catch him—or perhaps he's moved on and we will have no more murders."

Julie shuddered. "I can't believe that a monster can just stop," she said. "But I didn't feel any threat from the men who spoke to me last night—and none of them tried to get me to go off alone with them."

"Shall we carry on again tonight, then?" asked Dr. Watson.

"For as long as we have the energy," answered Holmes. "Eventually, we will have to get a few solid nights' sleep."

The rest of the day was very busy. The suspect list continued to dwindle, and Holmes distributed an updated list to the men. Everyone had been working so hard as well as interviewing the various drunks and crackpots who came in to confess.

Holmes' personal list read as follows:

- Joseph Barnett

Barnett is an out-of-work fishmonger who fits the physical description of the Ripper. He lived with Mary Jane Kelly for roughly a year (though not consistently) before her murder, and is known to have been angry she made her living on the streets.

Reasons to suspect Joseph Barnett as a suspect: He has knowledge and skill with knives and fits the description of the Ripper; he also likely has a key to Mary Jane's room, and thus could have easily let himself in without raising suspicion. Additionally, Mary Jane may not have initially struggled or fought against a man who she recognized as a lover, making it easy for him to overpower her.

- George Hutchinson

Hutchinson claims to be a witness who saw the last victim with a man shortly before her murder. He claims he came close enough to see the man's features and hear his voice. He saw the alleged murderer hand the woman a red handkerchief. However, there are several details that he should have noticed and did not. He followed the couple to Mary Jane's residence and waited outside, watching.

Reasons to consider George Hutchinson as a suspect: He could be Jack the Ripper, giving himself an alibi—however, he is the least likely suspect on the list.

- James Kelly

See notes on previous list. Kelly remains a strong suspect.

- George Chapman

See notes on previous list. Chapman remains a strong suspect.

- Dr. Alexander Pedachenko

Very little is known about Pedachenko, other than that he knew two of the victims.

Reasons to consider Dr. Alexander Pedachenko as a suspect: An informant has revealed Pedachenko may have been sent by the Russian police to commit these murders and discredit Scotland Yard, who the Russians believed to be too easy on socialists. Pedachenko is said to be a surgeon and enjoy wearing women's clothing; his motivation for the murders may have been exacerbated by mental illness.

- Francis Thompson

Francis Thompson, though he comes from a well-respected family, is an opium addict given to hallucinations—he has no known address and perhaps lives on the streets. We have been unable to interview him about the crimes, though we continue to seek his whereabouts.

Reasons to consider Francis Thompson as a suspect: Thompson is known to interact with prostitutes, as well as other less savory members of society; he has a habit of wearing neckties, and the victims may have been strangled with a necktie. He has worked in a medical factory and has had some surgical training, He also was allegedly in the vicinity of the murders at the time they occurred, and more than one witness has mentioned his instability and tendency toward violent anger. His physical description fits that given by other witnesses, as well.

- Francis Tumblety

An eccentric who presents himself as a physician and has knowledge of human anatomy. His housekeeper claims to have found bloody sheets in his house, and he lives in the area.

Reasons to consider Francis Tumblety as a suspect: Tumblety has the reputation as a woman hater, and dislikes prostitutes in particular. He has a collection of wombs and a history of violence.

- Alois Szemeredy

Szemeredy is a Hungarian surgeon who has served time in a lunatic asylum and has a history of violent crime, as well as a penchant for surgical knives. He resides in a hotel near where the crimes were committed, but we have been unable to interview him thus far in the investigation.

Reasons to consider Alois Szemeredy as a suspect: Szemeredy has a professed hatred of prostitutes and his past indicates an inclination toward mental instability and the capacity for murder. However, it appears the links between Szemeredy and the Ripper's crimes are weak without more information.

- Dr. John Williams

See notes on previous list; remains a suspect but is unlikely to be the Ripper.

Now, most certainly, Jack was amongst these people left on the list. The real work was about to begin...

CHAPTER NINETEEN
Intuition

As the sun began to set, Grant told Holmes they would have to put off the nights' surveillance due to unforeseen circumstances. He and the other officers would be working on another case. It appeared there was a lull in the murders, and other crimes on the London streets demanded attention.

Holmes was pleased with this turn of events, as he was eager to carry out the investigation on his own. He quickly decided that he and Dr. Watson, as well as Julie, would still visit the bar that night; Holmes wanted to observe the patrons and their habits.

Holmes left Scotland Yard and paid a call upon Julie. She was in, and answered the door herself—her humble home was a far cry from the orderly, upper-class address of Baker Street.

"Detective Holmes," she said with real pleasure in her voice—she liked the man, despite his many awkward quirks. "Will we still be trying to catch the Ripper tonight, or have you come with other plans?"

"Inspector Grant and the officers cannot join us tonight," Holmes said. "But Dr. Watson and I would still like to accompany you to Whitechapel—I assure you that we will not leave you unprotected."

"Of course. Anything I can do to catch this beast I will do," she told him.

"We won't be far from you, as I have said, so you will be safe. I have a notion that this might be the night," he said. "I want you to know how much I appreciate your help."

"And I yours. Please, come in—can I offer you anything?"

Holmes knew it was untoward to see Julie without a chaperone present—such things would start a torrent of gossip in proper society—but in Julie's neighborhood it was unlikely anyone would raise an eyebrow. He gladly accepted, and they sat in her small parlor and discussed the case.

"It's time for him to kill again isn't it?" Julie asked.

"Yes. This is Saturday night. It seems he only kills on the weekends, or so far anyway. Inspector Grant believes he is in a lull, or has moved on—but I have an intuition this is not the case. We will all have to be on our toes tonight."

"I certainly will," Julie laughed, a touch of cynicism in her tone. "Otherwise it's my head."

Holmes knew he needed to go talk to Dr. Watson, so he bid Julie farewell and left.

When Holmes arrived at his friend's house, he was happy to see there was a late lunch awaiting him. They sat down at the table and ate ham sandwiches with a mug of ale.

"So, we will be on our own tonight?" Dr. Watson asked.

"Yes, my friend. I hope that is alright with you."

"Quite so. We've always worked best alone. I do believe you know something you are not telling me yet. Am I right?"

"Well, let's just say I think I have a lead on the subject—as I have told you before."

"And I know you well enough to realize you will tell me nothing else, to preserve your objectivity. I know by now how you work, and I will do whatever you need me to do. We have to stick close to Julie."

The two men went over the suspect list. Dr. Watson knew the Ripper was on that list. Of course, there is always room for mistake, so they took each person seriously and went over the facts carefully.

"I still suspect there might be someone not on the list. I keep thinking Jack has a partner—an accomplice," Holmes said.

"That could be correct. We seem to have different descriptions along the way of what he looks like. Maybe one is luring the women to the real Ripper," Dr. Watson mused.

"Yes, that is a possibility. If there is an accomplice, Jack the Ripper could be anyone—perhaps no one has even set eyes on the fellow leading up to the crime. But if we can catch the accomplice, he might lead us to the bigger prize."

"Having an accomplice would also make easier the task of framing you," said Dr. Watson. "If more murders occur, it is only a matter of time before you are linked to one; and you will have only Mrs. Parker as an alibi."

"That worries me," Holmes admitted. "Mrs. Parker does not pay much attention to my comings and goings— she knows I cherish my privacy. That leads me back again to my theory of the secret society, one that opposes the Sovereign Order of the Count of Monte Cristo. It would be far easier for them to find a patsy to pin the crimes on me than it would be for an ordinary serial killer."

"The Sovereign Order of Monte Cristo is powerful,

though, my friend. Can't its members do something to help?"

"I have been hesitant to draw my old friend Dantes into this," answered Holmes. "He is a busy man with worries of his own. If the situation worsens and I am indeed linked to the crimes, I will not hesitate to reach out to him—but I still think we are close enough to capturing the Ripper that it won't be necessary."

"I shudder to think that any group of intelligent men—even those with reason to hate the Sovereign Order—would use innocent women as pawns against their enemies."

"I do as well, Watson. No civilized man would take such action. But then again, enemies of the Order may not have anything to do with this. Jack the Ripper might well be only one man, moved to do his horrible acts by inner conflict. We will just have to see how things play out."

CHAPTER TWENTY
Revelations

The man knew he had to go out that night. He readied himself and ran over in his mind what sort of woman he wanted to find. His blood pounded hotly in his veins, his heart beating faster with excitement. That killer instinct would not stop. He got such a thrill out of what he had been doing. Nobody was the wiser, and for all he knew, even though he might have been on Scotland Yard's suspect list, he wasn't a very viable one. He was smarter than that dumb detective, Holmes—otherwise Holmes would have caught him by now.

He stared at his somewhat stocky physique in the mirror—though often he lived on the streets, he now had enough money from his benefactors to rent a room whenever he wanted; he had also purchased some fine clothes. Though he was only of medium height, women seemed to find him attractive, even when he acted like an everyday bloke with no polish or education. The Ripper liked playacting. In his mind, all a woman really cared about was where her next dollar was coming from. Of course, many men merely wanted their manly urges satisfied, and whores were there for the taking. They were despicable cows doing anything for precious coin, and most of them were drunkards. If he was forced to admit it, most of them were harmless. This didn't matter to the Ripper.

Their insides were all the same. That he knew for sure. It was such a treat to get to see them from the inside out. Who would suspect him? What a thrill it gave him to feel their blood on his hands and the touch of innards sliding through his fingers—it was poetic, in a way. He didn't have sex with them. That did not interest him at all—only what they were and how they used their power over men. That's what mattered.

He must hurry and get ready. It was almost midnight. He had to make his appearance tonight, or those who now funded his lifestyle would be most displeased with him.

Out of the door he walked.

Julie was sitting at her place at the bar, attired in a black gown. She had arranged her hair in tumbling curls, atop which she had pinned a red and black hat. Multiple men approached her, offering a drink or something more, but she brushed them off—none of them fit the description of the man for whom she waited.

Holmes sat at a back corner table in disguise, while Dr. Watson lounged at the other end of the bar. They would not leave Julie unattended. Holmes had noticed three of the men on his suspect list in the bar that night. None of them had approached Julie, and all had left the bar alone. He was pretty sure none of them was the man he was looking for. Still…the night was young. Holmes remained hopeful.

Around 12:30 A.M. a short, stocky man, sharply dressed, walked in and took a place at the bar. He had been sitting for about half an hour when he looked over at Julie and nodded. She nodded back—he fit the description perfectly. Holmes and Dr. Watson watched him carefully, their bodies relaxed but their eyes bright and alert. This could be the one—Holmes was certain the man was one of the suspects on the list, though he couldn't be entirely sure in the dark bar.

The man eventually moved to a vacant stool next to Julie. They chatted for a while, Julie giggling and acting intoxicated. The man appeared to be entranced by her flirtatious behavior. He leaned over to whisper in her ear, and then steered her toward the door.

Julie's eyes searched for Holmes as she went with the man, but Holmes had already slipped outside. He had left as soon as the man started to pay his tab.

Julie and the stranger walked out onto the cobblestoned street, their heads inclined toward one another. Julie noticed that although the man's tone was relaxed, his body was tense—she sensed he was nervous. The street was lined with drunks and women of the night. Some of the prostitutes leaned in alcoves, quietly talking to men.

As Julie and her would-be suitor walked toward the end of the street, she was relieved to have spotted Holmes. Dr. Watson would not be far behind.

"What do you charge for a night of your companionship?" the man whispered in her ear.

"Well, it depends on what you want," Julie said, deliberately slurring her words a little. "I have to pay my bills, ya know—and if you haven't noticed, I am a beautiful woman. We don't come cheap."

"Let's walk down this alleyway here and discuss it."

"Whatever you say, darling," Julie said as she let herself be led down the dark street. "As long as you've got the coin to keep me, I'm yours."

They walked a ways down the alley, until the narrow passage expanded into a wider road. There were others in the vicinity, but none too close. The man guided Julie off of the path and into a dark corner of the street. All at once, he pulled up her skirts over her head and pushed. She fell at once to the ground and the glint of the knife shone in the moonlight.

"Stop!"

The man froze, his body tensed for flight.

"I said stop! And turn around."

The man slowly turned to face Holmes, who was pointing a pistol at him. Julie scrambled up and ran behind Holmes for protection.

"Well, we finally meet," the man said. "What took you so long, Inspector?"

"I had a feeling it was you, and I even think I know why you sought to frame me. You were on my list, I hope you know. I would have caught you in the end, even without tonight's subterfuge."

"I must respectfully disagree—I wasn't so sure you would catch me. Though now that you have, I must say I've had more fun than I imagined. This has been quite the sport for me."

The man was Francis Thompson, a poet and a writer. Exactly as Holmes had thought—though at first he had had trouble believing that a sensitive, intelligent man could commit such atrocities.

"It won't be so easy as you think to bring me to justice, however."

"Whatever do you mean? I have caught you red-handed—and I have a pistol, while you have only that knife. I think we both know who has the advantage here."

"Turn around," snapped another voice from behind Holmes.

As he turned, Holmes saw his friend, the coroner's

assistant Donald Hamilton, pointing a gun at him.

"Well, my friend. You quite surprise me, although I had a strange feeling about you. I suppose you are the one who left my personal effects at the murders. It was so easy for you to get to my desk, wasn't it? And I suppose into my home at well." Holmes waited for an answer.

"Yes, it was very easy. Almost laughably so."

"Why are you helping this lunatic?"

"It all happened quite innocently. I nearly caught him one night, and he needed a lookout. I couldn't turn down what he offered—and I was in the perfect position to help him. The pay has certainly been good."

Jack, or rather Francis, cleared his throat.

"Put down the pistol, Holmes. It appears the world's greatest detective has been outsmarted. Now, you will watch me punish this girl for your hubris—and then I will disappear. You will have it on your head, and I daresay the police may even begin to suspect you. Especially when I kill again, and leave something of yours on the body. I'm sure you received the little present I left on your desk—and you know I have other belongings of yours, as well. How careless of you to drop personal effects at the murder sites! I would never be so foolish." Francis laughed, an edge of mania in his voice.

Holmes did as he was told. The darkness enveloped them as Francis strode over and grabbed Julie by the arm to pull her back to him. At that exact moment, an arm came out of the darkness and snaked around Donald's neck. A loud crack sounded and Donald fell to the ground.

Holmes, Julie, and Francis turned to see what had happened. A smile crept over Holmes' face...

CHAPTER TWENTY-ONE
Dealing with the Devil

Dr. Watson stood behind where Donald had fallen. He had been in the military for many years and knew how to cleanly and efficiently snap a man's neck—without mess and without noise, just instant death. Though he regretted having another life on his hands, it had been the only way to save Holmes and Julie.

Holmes pointed the pistol at Francis once more. "Drop your knife and let Julie go," he commanded. Julie, shaking with fear, ran to Dr. Watson's side, keeping her eyes steadily away from Donald's body on the ground.

"Are you going to kill me?" said Francis, a coward now that his life was at stake.

"I still could," answered Dr. Watson. "But I know that my old friend has some questions he must ask you first."

Holmes nodded. "I suspect that your motivations are not merely the love of the kill—if my intuition serves me right, I would say you were sent by the Illuminati to destroy me because of my affiliation to the Sovereign Order of Monte Cristo. That is why you had Donald plant evidence linking me to the murders. Tell me it isn't so."

"Yes, you are correct. Killing two birds with one stone, so to speak. My benefactors paid me well, and I must say that with each murder I felt my creative powers growing. It was almost as if I'd been singled out by God—he gave me the key to unlock my gift. You should see how inspired I am after I kill—I write for hours! A man named Aaron Kosminksi approached me after my first murder—

he said he was with the Illuminati, and he thought we could have a mutually beneficial partnership. Just how the Illuminati figured out the first murder was mine I will never know—but Kosminksi offered me a handsome sum to begin leaving clues that pointed to you. It made no difference to me whether or not you were caught—and I must say I grew to enjoy it. Murder is a delicious thrill—as perhaps your dangerous Dr. Watson knows."

"There is a difference between slaughtering the innocent and protecting the ones we love," interrupted Dr. Watson stiffly. "We are not the same."

"Perhaps—perhaps. Tell me, though—how did you figure out the killer was me? There must have been more obvious suspects to investigate."

"Once I began thinking that the Illuminati was behind not the murders themselves, but rather was behind my personal effects being left at the murders, I started to look at the situation quite differently," Holmes explained. "I asked myself if there was some connection between the murders besides the mutilation, but it wasn't until my housekeeper mentioned lighting a candle to St. Raymond for her daughter that I began to piece it together. You see, her daughter is with child and she lit the candle to pray for her daughter's continued health; when I asked her what day she had done so, she told me August 31. The feast day of St. Raymond fell on the day of the first murder—and St. Raymond is also the patron saint of innocence. How ironic, to murder a prostitute on that day!"

A smile began to spread across Francis' face.

Holmes continued, "I then researched other saint days, and I realized that the other murders fell on symbolic days as well—Annie's murder was committed on the feast day of the patron saint of butchers, while Liz and Catherine were killed on the feast day for the patron saint of doctors. More damningly, each body was left in a place that would once have been considered a place of sanctuary—land surrounding a chapel that would provide safe haven for the accused."

Dr. Watson seemed to have forgotten where he was—he was listening to Holmes intently, fascinated. "And how on earth did you connect this to the Illuminati?" Dr. Watson asked.

"The Illuminati has long been dedicated to working against the Catholic Church," Holmes answered. "This would have been just their sort of clever joke—one that very few people would perceive. And now I see how Kosminski fits in as well—do you remember the message on the apron, Dr. Watson?"

"Yes!" Dr. Watson said, realization lighting up his eyes. "'*The juwes are the men who will not be blamed for nothing*'—how strange I thought that, and now I understand!"

"That tells me how you connected the Illuminati to the murders," interrupted Francis, "but not me."

"I am getting to that," answered Holmes. "One of the witnesses mentioned you to me as someone to interview; she told me you lived as a vagrant, though you had a privileged background, and said that very little happened on the streets of Whitechapel that you didn't know about. In my search for you, I discovered you are an opium addict, given to hallucinations—and your sister even gave me a box of writings you left behind when I wrote to her inquiring about your whereabouts. In that box were some very disturbing stories and poems—and in them you write passionately about disemboweling women, in the same manner the victims were killed. And yet the stories were obviously written before the murders occurred. When I also learned you had studied to be a surgeon, I realized I had identified the killer.

"But I still needed to know this beyond a doubt—and so I turned to the method I originally thought would be the key to solving the crime, fingerprint analysis. You see, iodine fumes reveal prints on paper—and I had the postcard and note left at my house. Though I was not able to lift a print off the bodies, I did find a bloody print in Mary Jane's room that appeared to match that on the missives. I had your writings as well, and the prints there connected it all together."

"It is rare a man has the ambition to turn his greatest fantasy into reality," said Francis. "Yet I have done so in my work as Jack the Ripper. Those writings are juvenile— I have grown immensely in talent since, and I should have burned them. I shall, if I can get my hands on them again. I cannot believe it was something so simple that led you conclusively to me!"

"Now it is my turn to ask a question," said Holmes. "Why murder prostitutes, rather than any woman you found alone in the street?"

Francis lost his smile at this question, and his lips curled into a snarl. "Because they are vile, lying trash," he said. "Once, I believed I had found the love of my life— and I begged her to leave the streets, and let me take care of her. She would take my money willingly enough, but would not agree to become my wife—and eventually I heard she had been mocking me openly behind my back. True, she was older than I—and society may never have accepted our love—she broke my heart. I do not know where she has gone, but I hope she reads of these murders and cannot sleep at night from fear."

"The last piece of the puzzle," muttered Holmes.

"So do you now march me to Scotland Yard, to bask in the glory of catching Jack the Ripper?" Francis said with a sneer.

"I have a deal to make with you," Holmes said as he glanced at Dr. Watson's forlorn face. "I do not want Dr. Watson to have to go through the rest of his life being publicly saddled with the death of this trash who lies before us. I also want the Illuminati to leave me alone, as well as my friend the Count of Monte Cristo," Holmes said. "You have to make them stop. Do you have the power to do that?"

"Yes, I believe I do," Francis said warily. "I know many of their names and they will not want to be associated with me. They are people in high places."

"If we reach an agreement, we must not ever mention this night to anyone. We will leave Donald's body to be found by someone else. You will return to your family, leaving London, and try to live the rest of your life out of the public eye," Holmes continued. "You will resume life as a poet and scholar, and will devote your writings to some safer subject—God, perhaps. If I see similar crimes being perpetrated in our fair country, I will not hesitate to send a tip to the authorities of any city in which you reside. You must stop this madness."

"You would set free a murderer to save your friends?" Francis asked. "How can you be sure I will keep my word?"

"I cannot—but I know you are a smart man, and probably wish to spend the remainder of your life pursuing your art, rather than finding yourself at the end of a hangman's noose. Of course, you will have to find some less violent source of inspiration. I, myself, will write an account of what has happened tonight. It will be sealed and left among my belongings, with the instructions that the letter is not to be opened for one hundred years after my death. Then the world will find out the truth about Jack the Ripper."

Holmes still had his pistol pointed directly at Francis. A savage, dark part of him wanted to pull the trigger and bring justice to the murder victims—but Holmes knew that Dr. Watson and Edmond Dantes would be better served by letting Francis go free. He could leverage Francis to blackmail the Illuminati, and protect them all— at least for a while.

Holmes slipped the gun inside the pocket of his overcoat, but kept his hand upon it and the barrel pointed at Francis. "Though you have proved yourself to be no gentleman, I trust you not to betray our agreement," said Holmes. "You will leave tomorrow—you will think of some clever excuse, I am sure, for your hasty return home—and then we shall never hear from you again. And you will write to those men you know in the Illuminati, as well, and threaten to reveal them if they ever again attempt to besmirch my character, or that of Edmond Dantes. Dr. Watson, please escort Julie home and return home yourself—I will see Francis to the station and help him procure a passage to his parents' home."

Holmes had more complex reasons for waiting with Francis as the sun rose than merely making sure he left London—he wanted first-hand insight into the mind of a serial killer who would speak freely, as there was no consequence for his crimes. And speak freely Francis did, describing each murder in detail and with relish. Holmes listened intently, though at times the man's twisted nature sent chills down his spine. Holmes learned that most of the details in his profile had been perceptive and correct, though a few were disproven.

When he had seen Francis off, Holmes knew he must return to work. He had to think about what to say to Grant. He guessed the investigation would have to go on for a while longer, even though there would be no more murders. Scotland Yard would not be convinced the Ripper's reign of terror had ended for quite some time, he was sure. Holmes would also have to coordinate a story with Julie and Dr. Watson, but he trusted them implicitly and had no doubt this secret could be kept for one hundred years—as long as Francis did not take up the Ripper's sharp knife once more.

EPILOGUE

Dr. Watson sat in his den, going over the night's happenings. Though he had killed men in the war, those deaths still haunted him, and he regretted adding another man's life to his list of transgressions. He had to protect his old friend, however, as well as the innocent Julie. He would live with his remorse and keep the secret—after all, Donald Hamilton was almost as evil a man as the Ripper himself, and the world was well rid of him.

Julie had surprised Dr. Watson by thanking him for helping to avenge her friend's death—she appeared to have no ill effects from the night's misadventures at all, and if she disagreed with Holmes' decision to send Francis away rather than having him hanged, she did not say it. Dr. Watson closed his eyes against the bright morning sun, hoping that his old friend was safe and that he would hear from him soon.

Holmes went home, his body weary and his head aching. He knew he would not find the sweet peace of rest for quite some time—there were details to be taken care of at Scotland Yard. He was hungry though, and needed to bathe and change his clothes. His trusty housekeeper was there to make his breakfast and not ask questions. She had learned by now that he preferred her conversation to remain focused on trivial matters, and for her hands to stay busy keeping his coffee cup full.

While Holmes dressed for the day, she made him a breakfast of pancakes and scrambled eggs along with fresh sausage. She poured a cup of coffee for him as well. They made small talk as he ate and then prepared to leave. She knew she would probably not see him until that evening. He looked like a man with a purpose.

Scotland Yard was buzzing with excitement. A body had been found. Yes, the body of one of the employees of the coroner's office.

"Have you heard the news about Donald Hamilton?" asked Grant as soon as Holmes strode into the office.

"Just now—and I must tell you I am shocked."

"I do not think our murderer was the Ripper, unless Hamilton caught the fellow in the act and the woman fled and hasn't come forward yet. The fellow had his neck broken—snapped clean. It had to be the work of some sort of professional I am sure, and a strong one at that. We have no clues to go on yet, but we will of course investigate every avenue."

"I hate to hear this news," Holmes said, shaking his head. "He seemed like such a nice young man, with a bright future ahead of him. Were there any witnesses?"

"No, not a one. A merchant delivering eggs found the body hidden in an alley. Your priority will remain the Ripper case, of course. Will we be returning to Whitechapel with Julie tonight?"

"Let us revisit our strategy over the next fortnight," answered Holmes. "As it is no longer the weekend, the Ripper is unlikely to kill—and Julie has withdrawn from the investigation. The night's excitement in the pub proved too much for her nerves. And perhaps there will be no more murders—perhaps London is finally through with this madness."

Grant agreed with Holmes' request to postpone their next visit to Whitechapel, though with some hesitation—he knew Holmes was not a man to let go of a case until it was solved, and he did not understand his friend's sudden withdrawal. Nevertheless, he was sure Holmes had some brilliant new tactic that he was not ready to share just yet.

Holmes knew he could not just halt his investigation and the investigations of all of the other detectives. He would have to play along for a while, and give the appearance of being devoted to solving the murders. He knew that after a few weeks, the excitement and terror would begin to fade, the trail would go cold, and the files would grow dusty as Scotland Yard moved on to other matters.

Though Holmes secretly longed for the world to know that he had, indeed, captured the world's most notorious serial killer, his devotion to his friends and the Sovereign Order of Monte Cristo overcame his pride—he had protected those he cared about, which was more important than adding another great investigatory feat to his reputation.

Maybe Jack the Ripper murders would not be solved for at least one hundred years…on that he would bet his last farthing.

THE END

ABOUT THE AUTHOR

Who is The Holy Ghost Writer?

The identity of the author is part of an international contest, and the first person to correctly name the HG Writer from the clues found in the Count of Monte Cristo sequels will receive a reward of $5000. Visit the Holy Ghost Writer's Amazon Author Page for Details and see if you can discover the real identity of the author being heralded as the new Stieg Larsson for That Girl Started Her Own Country, the successor of Alexander Dumas for The Sultan of Monte Cristo and the next Ray Bradbury for The Boy Who Played With Dark Matter. Contact the author c/o books@illuminatedpublications.com

CPSIA information can be obtained at www.ICGtesting.com
Printed in the USA
LVOW10s1933250215

428338LV00033B/1761/P